FIGS. 73—75 COAL-TIT.   FIGS. 91 PIED WAGTAIL.   FIGS. 102 ROCK-PIPIT.
     76—77 MARSH-TIT.   92 WHITE WAGTAIL.   103 GOLDEN ORIOLE.
     78—81 BLUE TIT.   93 GREY WAGTAIL.   104—108 RED-BACKED SHRIKE.
        82 CRESTED TIT.   94 BLUE-HEADED WAGTAIL.   109 WOODCHAT SHRIKE.
     83—84 NUTHATCH.   95—96 YELLOW WAGTAIL.   110 PIED FLYCATCHER.
     85—87 WREN.   97—100 TREE-PIPIT.   111—113 SPOTTED FLYCATCHER.
     88—90 TREE CREEPER.   101 MEADOW-PIPIT.

THE WREN

Wren

THE WREN

A BIOGRAPHY

The Secret Life of Britain's
Most Common Bird

STEPHEN MOSS

■ SQUARE PEG

1 3 5 7 9 10 8 6 4 2

Square Peg, an imprint of Vintage,
20 Vauxhall Bridge Road,
London SW1V 2SA

Square Peg is part of the Penguin Random House group of companies whose
addresses can be found at global.penguinrandomhouse.com.

Penguin
Random House
UK

Text copyright © Stephen Moss 2018

Stephen Moss has asserted his right to be identified as the author of this Work
in accordance with the Copyright, Designs and Patents Act 1988

First published by Square Peg in 2018

Penguin.co.uk/vintage

A CIP catalogue record for this book is available from the British Library

ISBN 9781910931936

Typeset by Dinah Drazin

Printed and bound by C&C Offset Printing Co., Ltd

Penguin Random House is committed to a sustainable future for our
business, our readers and our planet. This book is made from
Forest Stewardship Council® certified paper.

To Mike Dolan, my father-in-law,
who has a soft spot for wrens

Wren

Cock-tailed gobshite in the thorn.
Flitter-tongue, shrew, shrill tocsin,
tilt-arse, bustle, creep-a-mouse,
brownblur, blownburr, bellower, bumfluff,
jitterbug, puffball, alarum, pocket rooster,
songbag, waggledance, autumn bauble,
spew-a-jewel, dumpling, sinew-buster,
cordite, fizzgig, Billy Fury.
Apoplectic vol-au-vent.

Steven Lovatt

NANNUS TROGLODYTES LIN.   REGULUS REGULUS LIN.

Gärdsmyg.   *Kungsfågel 1 ♂, 2 ♀.*

INTRODUCTION

He who shall hurt the little wren
Shall never be beloved by men.

William Blake, 'Auguries of
Innocence', c. 1803

On a bright, cold winter's day, as I look out of the kitchen window soon after sunrise, I notice the usual flurry of activity on the bird feeders.

Great tits, resplendent in black and yellow, trade places with their smaller cousins the blue tits, each momentarily pausing to grab a seed before flying off. There's a male chaffinch – with salmon-pink underparts and smart white flashes on his wings. And a flock of goldfinches, whose yellow wing-bars and crimson faces make them one of the most striking of all our garden birds.

On the bird table itself, a cock blackbird tilts his head to reveal his golden eye-ring while, on the ground below, a robin feeds on scattered seeds, showing off his famous red breast.

But there is another garden bird here today: one that is less colourful, far less showy, and very easy to miss. I can see it now, quiet and unassuming, lurking deep in the shadows beneath the shrubbery, like a shy actor waiting in the wings while others take centre stage. It hops from one spot to the next, its sudden, jerky movements reminding me more of a small mouse than a bird. Yet a bird it is: a wren.

Whenever I encounter a wren, it is always a welcome sight: a reassuringly familiar presence, like bumping into an old friend. And I come across them often. Indeed, almost everywhere I travel in the British Isles, from the heart of London to the remotest offshore island, I know that I shall find wrens.

I have heard them in city parks and suburban gardens, in picturesque English villages and by majestic Scottish lochs. I have found them in woodland, hedgerows, and on the edge of farmland. I have seen them perching on top of a gorse bush on a baking-hot southern heath, and sheltering in the heather on a blustery northern moor. I have come across wrens hopping about on bleak and windswept coastal headlands, and have even seen one on the snowy slopes of the Cairngorm mountains.

And yet when I tell people that the wren is Britain's commonest bird, they often express surprise – even disbelief. Many confess, rather shamefacedly, that they have never even seen a wren. But, given that there are about eight million breeding pairs in these islands, they have probably been within a few yards of one more times than they could imagine.

In some ways, it is rather odd that so many people are unaware of a creature that is all around them; hidden, as it were, in plain sight. It's not as if wrens can be easily confused with any other bird. No other species has that distinctive stumpy shape and cocked tail, making the wren straightforward to identify, even in silhouette.

Wrens do tend to skulk along the ground, it's true; but, especially in winter and early spring, they are also very active. Perhaps it's because they rarely stay in the same place or position for more than a second or two, before flying off on those short, whirring wings. Not so much shy and elusive, as they are often described, but simply fast and furious. As the *Guardian* Country Diarist Thomas Coward pointed out back in the 1920s, 'Poets and sentimentalists talk of the shy and retiring Wren; really it is indifferent to our presence.'

Having discovered that Britain's most numerous species of bird has been eluding them for so long, most people are keen to know more. So let me tell you about the feisty little wren, and its remarkable lifestyle.

At nine or ten centimetres (three-and-a-half to four inches) long, and weighing just ten grams (roughly one-third of an ounce), the wren is often thought of as Britain's smallest bird.

Yet despite its diminutive size, the wren is beaten to that title by the goldcrest and firecrest, which are both marginally shorter, and about half the wren's weight, tipping the scales at just five grams (barely one-sixth of an ounce). Even so, a wren only weighs the same as two sheets of A4 paper, or a shiny new one-pound coin.

But statistics cannot really do justice to this little ball of energy. Writers down the ages have attempted to sum up the wren's character in a word or phrase, such as 'businesslike', 'vigorous and active', 'dumpy and energetic' and, my favourite, 'tiny, restless and pugnacious', coined by the godfather of British birding, Ian Wallace.

Yet none of these quite manages to capture the wren's true nature. The Victorian nature writer W. H. Hudson perhaps came closest when he wrote of:

The little nut-brown wren – nut-like, too, in his smallness and round, compact figure – with cocked-up tail and jerky motions and

gesticulations, and flight as of a fairy-partridge with rapidly-beating, short wings, that produce a whirring noise if you are close enough to hear it...

A multitude of folk-names also reflect the nature of this captivating little bird. The French lexicographer Michel Desfayes lists well over a hundred different local names for the wren in Britain, the vast majority of which derive from the bird's small size and compact shape.

These include titty and tittywren (along with variants such as cutty-wren, chitty-wren and tiddly-creeper); tomtit and tom-in-the-wall – in which 'tom' signifies something small, as in the children's fairytale 'Tom Thumb'; two-fingers, another reference to its small size; and stumpy, stumpit and stumpy-dick, all of which refer to the wren's most prominent feature, its characteristically sticking-up tail.

Along with two other garden favourites, the Robin redbreast and

Tom tit, the wren also boasts a number of affectionate monikers based on our own Christian names, including Kitty wren, Bobby wren and, the best-known, Jenny wren – a name still occasionally used by members of the older generation. Such names were once far more prevalent: writing in the 1860s, the egg collector J. C. Atkinson remarked that 'I scarcely ever remember to have spoken of the Wren, or heard others speak of it, without some gentle, loving epithet being applied to its name.'

When it comes to its scientific name, the wren is famously burdened with the tongue-twister *Troglodytes troglodytes*, which derives from the Latin for 'cave-dweller'. As the early nineteenth-century ornithologist George Montagu pointed out, this might more fittingly be applied to any one of a number of hole-nesting species, such as the kingfisher or sand martin. I suspect that the name actually refers to the wren's habit of exploring nooks and crannies in ivy or dry-stone walls, rather than having anything to do with caves.

And what of the name 'wren' itself? Like so many of our oldest and most longstanding bird names, its origins remain a puzzle. The philologist W. B. Lockwood believed that the name's roots were in West Germanic, the ancestor of English, German and Dutch, which was spoken in an area stretching from the Alps to the North Sea around the time of Christ's birth. He went on to suggest that the name refers to the bird's cocked tail, though I'm not sure this was anything more than an educated guess.

According to the American anthropologist Elizabeth Atwood Lawrence, who made a special study of the folklore surrounding the wren, the bird's name has sexual connotations, linking the characteristically upright tail to a human erection.

*

For such a small, secretive and often overlooked bird, the wren looms surprisingly large in our culture, literature and folklore. Wrens feature in the writings of many of the greats of English Literature: from Chaucer and Shakespeare, through John Dryden, William Blake and John Clare to the comic verse of Edward Lear:

> two owls and a hen,
> four larks and a wren,
> have all built their nests in my beard.

Wrens also appear in a plethora of folk tales and rhymes, often paired with the robin, as 'God Almighty's cock and hen'.

But our relationship with the wren has a darker side, too. The rather grisly ritual of the Wren Hunt, for some while a custom in parts of western Britain and Ireland, traditionally took place on St Stephen's Day (26 December), and involved bands of young men and boys wandering around their village in pursuit of a wren which, once captured, was paraded around in a cage for all to see, and then killed.

Wrens feature in other aspects of our history and culture, too. In 1937, the image of a plump, cock-tailed wren displaced Britannia on the farthing (worth a quarter of an old penny), and remained there until our smallest coin was finally taken out of circulation in 1960.

The Women's Royal Naval Service was founded in 1917 and, although it was disbanded after the end of hostilities in 1919, re-formed at the start of the Second World War. Given its acronym WRNS, it didn't take long before this brave and pioneering band of women were dubbed 'the Wrens'. A less salubrious nickname goes back to the Crimean War, when prostitutes serving the soldiers based in County Kildare, Ireland, were known as 'wrens', because they 'do not live in houses . . . but build for themselves "nests" in the bush'.

Later in this book, I shall delve deeper into the fascinating folklore surrounding this species, exploring the many stories, folk tales, rhymes, songs and poems that it has inspired over the centuries. But first, let's return to the real wren, back in my Somerset garden.

Early one morning, I notice a wren emerge from beneath the shrubbery, and then hop up onto a low wall, pausing for a moment or two for me to admire him. Although from a distance wrens usually appear to be plain brown, once he comes into full view I can finally appreciate the subtleties of his beautifully patterned plumage.

My first impression, using only my naked eye, is of a warm brown shade, but a closer look through my binoculars reveals that each individual feather is edged with buff, black or grey, creating a subtle, barred effect. Above his eyes, he sports a narrow, pale stripe (known as the supercilium), contrasting with a darker stripe running from the base of the bill through the centre of each eye. His breast, belly and flanks are paler buff, and are less strongly marked than the back, wings and tail.

Watching him at such close range, I can also appreciate the wren's classic features. He has a long, thin, marginally downcurved bill, ideal for picking off tiny insects as he forages through the leaf-litter; short, stumpy wings, barely projecting past his body; and long, spring-loaded legs. Most obvious of all is that distinctively cocked tail, which is lowered into a horizontal position when he takes to the air.

Then, just as quickly as this bird arrived, he heads off, a blur of wings. In the words of Ian Wallace, 'in flight . . . it becomes just a compact, round-winged, almost bee-like creature.' Less than a minute has passed, yet I feel an immense sense of privilege; for unlike our other garden birds, wrens rarely stay in one place for very long, and hardly ever allow such close and prolonged views.

It is almost as if a wren knows that because it lives such a brief life, it must, in Rudyard Kipling's words, fill every 'unforgiving minute with sixty seconds' worth of distance run' – or in this case, flown.

Even though the wren is so common, so widespread and, for those of us who are aware of its presence, so familiar, it is still not an easy bird to get to know. I have watched – or perhaps I should say I have been aware of – wrens for close to half a century, since I first noticed one in my suburban childhood garden, some time in the late 1960s.

Everywhere I have lived since, from the centre of London to the city of Cambridge, and now in the heart of rural Somerset, wrens have been my constant companions. And yet I have been as guilty as anyone else of not paying them the attention they deserve.

I say 'anyone else', but I must make one exception: the man who studied the wren's habits and life cycle more closely than any other person, before or since: Edward Armstrong.

The Revd Edward Allworthy Armstrong was born in the first year of the twentieth century, in Belfast (now in Northern Ireland). Described as 'bald, meticulous, with a perpetual sense of wonder', Armstrong studied philosophy and psychology in Belfast before moving to Cambridge, where he took holy orders. Having worked for two decades in Hong Kong and Yorkshire, he then returned to the leafy suburbs of Cambridge, as Vicar of St Mark's Church, Newnham, in 1943.

Towards the end of that turbulent and eventful year in our nation's history, Armstrong experienced the epiphany that would change the course of his life. He described the moment in the introduction to his masterful Collins New Naturalist monograph, *The Wren*:

> Darkness was falling on a November evening . . . and the bombers were roaring off into the gloom when, happening to look out of my study window, I saw a small bird alight on the trellis outside and then fly up into the ivy on the wall. A couple of evenings later the wren was there again. . . My interest was again captured by a bird which had fascinated me as a boy. Here was a species about which I should like to know more.

Like David Lack and his beloved robins, Armstrong initially chose to study the wren for reasons of convenience. Strict wartime petrol rationing was in force, which made travel difficult, if not impossible. And having just begun a new job, with new responsibilities towards his flock of parishioners, Armstrong could hardly afford the time to venture farther afield in search of a more exotic subject.

But there was another, deeper impulse behind his choice of the wren. By focusing on the local and familiar, and attempting to unravel the secrets of just one of God's multitude of creatures, he was following in a long and distinguished tradition of holy men connected with the natural world, going all the way back to St Francis of Assisi. Armstrong himself made no such claim, though he did venture to compare himself with another famous vicar: 'Perhaps I could make the best use of my meagre opportunities if I were to concentrate on studying the "life and conversation," as Gilbert White would have put it, of a single species.'

And that's exactly what Edward Armstrong did. By the time he died in 1978, the same age as the century, he was hailed as one of the last of a long line of 'parson-naturalists', going back to Gilbert White himself. And despite – or perhaps because of – his lack of any formal scientific training, he produced a masterpiece about one of Britain's most overlooked birds, the humble wren.

As we have already seen, the subject of his lifelong studies, and of this more modest book, is something of a paradox. A bird that may at first glimpse seem ordinary and undistinguished – even, perhaps, uninspiring – turns out to be far more fascinating than we could ever have imagined.

Just as a close examination of the wren's plumage reveals something far more interesting than just 'brown', so looking further into its habits and behaviour also produces some amazing revelations.

No other British bird, for example, builds up to half-a-dozen different 'cock's nests' for the fussy female to examine, before she chooses the ideal 'des res' where she and her mate can settle down and raise a family. No other bird combines a mostly sedentary nature with the ability to conquer a wider range of habitats than virtually any other species, anywhere in the world. And no other small bird – with the possible exception of Cetti's warbler – has quite such a loud song for its small size.

The wren's sound is another important aspect of its character. For even when someone claims that they have never seen a wren, when I play them a recording of the bird's loud and distinctive song, full of tweets and trills, warblings and arpeggios, they usually recognise it.

When he sings, the cock wren will shake his wings and move from side to side on those springy legs. It's almost as if he cannot contain the sheer energy within his tiny body, as he releases it through this sudden burst of sound – memorably described by one observer as 'a dance of rainbows'.

Such showiness may seem paradoxical for a bird that keeps hidden away for so much of its life. And yet for me, it sums up the wonder of the wren. It is another reason why, after writing a study of Britain's favourite bird, the robin, I decided to focus on our commonest, yet also one of our least familiar, species.

Now it's time for the wren to come out from its hiding place, and emerge into the limelight, so that we can take a proper look at this abundant, yet mysterious, bird.

Stephen Moss

Mark, Somerset
April 2018

Wren

JANUARY

Wren, *n*.

One or other species of small passerine birds belonging to the genus *Troglodytes*, esp. the common wren, native to Europe.

Oxford English Dictionary

Several million years ago, deep in the heart of what is now North America, a bird began to sing.

It was a winter wren, a close cousin of our own familiar bird. But this particular wren was different. He was a pioneer: the first of his long line of descendants to strike out on his own, at the start of an epic journey. This journey would ultimately lead to the wren becoming one of the most successful of all the world's 10,000 or so species of bird.

What impelled this tiny creature to leave the riverside forest where he was born, and begin to head north and west, we simply don't know. Perhaps there were just too many of his fellow wrens competing for too little food and breeding territories, in too small a space. Or maybe he had undergone a small but significant genetic mutation that turned him from a sedentary lifestyle towards a nomadic one.

Whatever the initial impulse, he continued to follow the spring sun. He was not the only one: other wrens – males and females – had begun to explore new lands too. As they flew northwards, the days lengthened, the competition from rivals grew less intense, and he was finally able to settle down, find a mate, and between them raise a healthy brood of six chicks.

Soon afterwards, he died – killed by a passing hawk. But his offspring had inherited the blueprint that drove them to be adventurous too. Gradually, over hundreds, perhaps thousands, of generations, these little birds spread themselves over the whole of the North American continent, until one intrepid individual found himself at the western fringes of present-day Alaska.

At that time, sea levels had dropped so low that there was a land bridge across what is now the Bering Strait, between Alaska and Siberia. So he crossed over this narrow isthmus of land, and became the first of his kind to reach the Old World. Over the next few thousand years, before the oceans finally parted these two great continents, successive generations of wrens followed the same path, entering the vast land-mass of Eurasia here, at its easternmost point.

But they didn't stop there. Over the next million years or so, they forged their route westwards, through vast forests, over ice-blue lakes and across winding rivers. Here, in the absence of competition from other very small birds, food and nesting places were abundant. That meant that the wrens could exploit their ability to feed on tiny insects ignored by larger birds, and nest anywhere with a suitable crevice, crack or cavity to conceal their eggs and chicks.

Time passed, and eventually the descendants of those wrens reached present-day Europe. Some then headed south, to make their home on the fringes of the Sahara Desert in North Africa, or in the equally arid lands of the Middle East; others stayed where they were, in the woods and forests of western Russia and Scandinavia.

But a handful of birds, driven by that innate ancestral desire to explore, continued on their journey. One autumn, helped by easterly winds, they managed to cross the North Sea, and began to spread throughout Britain, and later Ireland. Some got even further, as James

Fisher pointed out in his account of an epic journey across the US in *Wild America*: 'Even in Iceland there are wrens; their stubby wings and the wind have taken them seven-eighths of the way around the world.'

And so, over unimaginably long aeons of time, the wren spread from its original home in the New World, throughout huge swathes of the Old World, and almost came back full circle. Along the way, it achieved unprecedented success, becoming one of our commonest and most familiar birds.

In the west of the wren's present-day range, in the heart of rural England, a high-pressure system has arrived from the east. It has brought clear skies and windless nights, and the temperature has plummeted well below freezing. The snow that fell on New Year's Day has not yet begun to melt, spelling disaster for those birds that, like the wren, feed mainly on the ground. For a bird as small and light as this, these are desperate times, which call for desperate measures.

In one corner of the garden is a nest box, put up last autumn in preparation for the breeding season to come. It is designed for hole-nesting birds such as blue or great tits. But before they get the chance to move in, squatters have taken advantage of this temporary home.

Just before dusk, as the mercury begins to fall, a whirr of wings signals the arrival of a single wren. It perches momentarily on the low horizontal branch next to the box, delivers a short burst of song, and then flies straight in through the entrance hole.

Soon afterwards, another wren arrives, and also goes through the hole, followed by another, and then another. These early arrivals huddle together at the base of the box, where the temperature stays warmest, with any latecomers piling in on top of their sleeping bodies. Usually, roosts such as this will attract perhaps half a dozen birds, but on a freezing night during the winter of 1969, one observer in Norfolk counted the astonishing total of more than sixty wrens entering a single nest box.

As soon as daybreak approaches, they will all leave, squeezing back out through the hole one by one, to resume their individual lives. But when the weather gets this bad, a wren has no choice but to renounce its normally solitary existence, and 'buddy up' for the night – not just with one partner, but with as many as it can find.

At this time of year, each individual wren has a simple, clear and urgent mission: to survive. Like other small birds, wrens rarely live longer than a couple of years, with only one or perhaps two chances to breed. So getting through the winter is absolutely essential.

Most of our familiar garden birds are part of a larger family, with several species found here in Britain. We are home to half a dozen species of tit, a dozen different finches, and several thrushes, flycatchers and chats, the latter including two of our best-loved songsters, the nightingale and the robin.

But the wren stands alone, as not just the only member of its large and diverse family in Britain, but also the only one found across the whole of Europe and Asia. The wren we see in the British Isles – more properly called the Eurasian wren – is unique amongst Britain's birds, as it is the only species whose family has its origins in the New World rather than the Old. We may regard the wren as quintessentially British, but its family roots are way out west, on the other side of the Atlantic. Not so much a true Brit as an adopted Yank.

It turns out that 'our' wren is one of almost ninety different species in the family Troglodytidae, the rest of which are found exclusively in the

Americas. It is thought that they evolved in the forests of Central America, where the widest range of species can still be found today.

As a family, wrens are mostly small, brown and fairly inconspicuous, though often make up for this with their loud, complex and striking songs. Indeed, four species – the musician wren, the song wren, the flutist wren and the nightingale wren – are named for the beauty of the sounds they make.

The Eurasian wren is one of the smallest members of this large and varied clan, which also includes the Zapata wren, found only in a single swamp on the island of Cuba; the cactus wren, which makes its home in the prickly pears of the south-western United States; and the largest species, the aptly named giant wren, a thrush-sized bird confined to a tiny corner of Mexico.

Like the Eurasian wren, many species hold their tails up at a right angle to their body when perched, and are mostly insectivorous in their diet, picking off tiny insects and other invertebrates with their sharp, slender, pointed bills. They tend to hunt on or close to the ground, foraging in leaf litter, scrub and earth, where their food items are more numerous. Wrens often have quite short wings: not well suited to flying long distances, but ideal for a life spent amongst dense vegetation, where manoeuvrability is far more important.

In their original Western Hemisphere home, wrens remain one of the most widespread of all the bird families. They can be found from Alaska in the north to Tierra del Fuego in the south, and from sea level to altitudes of more than 3,300 metres (10,000 feet). That's largely because the food they need is also found in a very wide range of habitats: almost anywhere with ground vegetation is home to tiny insects, and so is ideal for wrens.

Wrens are sometimes polygynous – the male having more than one female during the same breeding season. Their nests tend to be quite complex structures, often almost entirely enclosed, apart from a small entrance for the parent birds to come in and out with food for the chicks. But only the female incubates the eggs. Outside the breeding season, wrens are usually solitary but, as we have seen, they will occasionally join forces with others in winter roosts, especially if the weather gets very cold.

Some species, such as the house wren – named because it often lives close to human habitation – have a vast geographic range. This common and familiar bird (now thought to be two closely related 'sibling species') can be found throughout virtually the whole of South and Central America, where it is sedentary; and in North America right up to the United States' border with Canada, where it is migratory. House wrens have been able to thrive across such a large area because – just like the Eurasian wren – they can exploit a very wide range of habitats, wherever they can find tiny insects on which to feed.

Another very widespread species of wren, found across much of eastern and central North America as far west as the Rocky Mountains, is the winter wren. Until just over a decade ago, this was considered to be the same species as the wrens we see in Britain. But with advances in genetics, scientists have now 'split' them into three species: the winter wren, the Pacific wren of western North America, and our own bird, renamed the Eurasian wren. Genetically they may be different, but the three species still look – and sound – remarkably similar, with more or less the same shape, colour and appearance, and a loud, high-pitched, trilling song.

Other kinds of wren are far more restricted in where they live. Several are confined to tiny islands, such as the Socorro and Cozumel wrens, found only on those eponymous specks of land off the western and eastern coasts of Mexico – where, despite their very restricted range, they are fairly common.

The same cannot be said for a trio of ultra-rare species found only in the eastern Andes Mountains of Colombia or neighbouring ranges in Venezuela. These are the recently rediscovered Santa Marta wren; Niceforo's wren, which went missing for almost fifty years until it was found again in 1989; and the Munchique wood-wren, which was not described by scientists at all until the early years of the twenty-first century.

All these species are on the verge of vanishing forever, as their homes are rapidly being degraded and destroyed by habitat loss. They are not the only ones: the conservation organisation BirdLife International classifies one in six of the world's wren species as being under threat of extinction.

So how, given that many of the Eurasian wren's cousins are so scarce and specialised, has the species we know and love managed to buck the trend so comprehensively? It comes down to two crucial aspects of the wren's life: its ability to live in a wide range of different habitats and geographical locations; and the pioneering nature that led this one species to break away from its sedentary relatives and conquer the Old World.

We often speak of birds being tied to a particular habitat, and to some extent that is the best way of explaining why some birds live where they do. If you were looking for a seabird, you'd naturally head for the coast; whereas if waterbirds were your target, then you'd visit a wetland.

But the sheer ubiquity of Eurasian wrens makes distinctions like this meaningless, as the definitive work on the birds of Britain, Europe, North Africa and the Middle East (*The Birds of the Western Palearctic*) points out:

> **Habitat**: Within predominantly moist mild climatic range, suitable habitat offered by variety of low cover and foraging opportunities, including herb and field layers of plant growth (within or outside woodland), crops and aquatic vegetation, fallen trees or heaps of brash, hedgerows, gardens, parks, and shrubberies. It is attracted to earthen banks, stone walls, outhouses and other free-standing structures, and natural crags, fissures, sea-cliffs, and other faces or slopes providing cavities, crevices, and interstices which can be profitably explored or used for roosting and nesting.

In other words, wrens can live virtually anywhere. The key to their survival throughout the year (as they tend to stay put at or near the

A.WAGNER

place where they were born) is a ready supply of insect food, available all year round.

Wrens are constantly active, searching for whatever they can find to eat, including spiders, beetles, mosquitoes, flies, ants and caterpillars. These almost invisible creatures can be found in almost any natural or man-made crevice; hence the huge variety of places where wrens are able to make their home. Unlike flying insects, which disappear when the weather turns cold, the creatures on which the wren feeds are always available; so, unlike birds such as the swallow, the majority of our wrens have no need to migrate.

You might imagine that the wren would not be the only species to rely on small insects, and you'd be right; but this is where the combination of its tiny size and long, slender bill really does pay off. No other British or European bird is able to exploit quite such a variety of ecological niches. That's because, apart from the goldcrest, which mostly lives and feeds in conifers, other species are simply too large to be able to survive entirely on such minuscule creatures.

As W. H. Hudson noted:

His activity, and habit of seeking his food in holes and dark places which are not explored by other insectivorous species, enable him to exist in a great variety of conditions – gardens, orchards, deep woods, open commons, hedgerows, rocky shores, swamps, mountains, and moors; there are, indeed, few places where the small, busy wren is not to be met with. This ability of the wren to find everywhere in nature a neglected corner to occupy would appear to give it a great advantage over other small birds.

Watch a wren as it goes about its foraging, and Hudson's description really does come to life. When feeding, wrens are the ultimate snackers. They move rapidly from one spot to the next, hopping from twig to twig and stone to stone, seizing any small morsels of food they come across on their travels. They are helped by having those springy legs, with long, curved claws, which enable the bird to cling onto the sides of buildings, or the bark of trees, and to move rapidly from one spot to another.

Their tiny size is also useful, enabling them to squeeze through gaps that would not allow a larger bird to enter. Like other small birds – and indeed small mammals such as mice, voles or shrews, which follow a very similar feeding strategy – wrens need to constantly replenish their energy. That's especially crucial on cold winter days, when the time and opportunities for feeding are so short. They do so by following a 'feeding circuit': a defined route where they know that they will find what they are looking for. So, even if a wren has vanished before your eyes, if you wait patiently, it will eventually return.

In terms of both space and time, a wren's world is on a very different level to ours, giving it a strikingly different perspective. Whereas we look at habitats on a landscape scale, the wren works on a much smaller canvas: within each microhabitat, it simply sees opportunities to find food, roost and nest.

As the giant of twentieth-century ornithology Max Nicholson noted in his 1951 book *Birds and Men*:

> A wren's world . . . is more comparable in some ways to a mouse's than to our own, and the wren cannot be adequately described as a bird of woodlands, gardens, fields, moors, marshes, cliffs or wastelands – although it is all of these – but must be looked at rather as a bird of crevices and crannies, of woodpiles and fallen trees, of hedge-bottoms and banks, walls and boulders, wherever these may occur. Wrens therefore can cut across, or rather scramble under, the imaginary boundaries which we are accustomed to draw between different types of country.

To a wren, any small patch of land – from a suburban garden to a hedgerow – provides a cornucopia of opportunities, so why would it ever choose to leave? Yet this raises an important question: if wrens are so sedentary (and those that live in the milder climates of lowland Britain generally are), then how on earth have they managed to reach more of our offshore islands than any other British bird?

This goes back to the wren's history as a successful colonist. Having crossed over from North America into Asia, when the descendants of those pioneering wrens finally reached the western extremities of the vast Eurasian landmass, they did not stop. Despite having short, stubby wings that make it look as if they could hardly fly further than the next bush, a few adventurous individuals managed to cross over from mainland Scotland and colonise the farthest fringes of the British Isles. And so today, wrens can be found in the Outer Hebrides, Shetland, Fair Isle and – way out in the Atlantic Ocean – the remotest archipelago of all, St Kilda.

After they had reached these islands, something truly astounding happened. These wrens developed their own unique characteristics, in response to their harsh and demanding new home. They grew larger, their colour and shade changed, and they altered their song too, over countless generations becoming different enough for scientists to classify them as four unique races or subspecies. (Confusingly, there is also another race, *indigenus*, that breeds in northern counties of England, while those in the south are of the nominate race *troglodytes*, making six in all.)

They were not the only ones. The Eurasian wren has a vast range, from Iceland in the west to Kamchatka and Japan in the east, and from beyond the Arctic Circle in the north to the edge of the Sahara Desert in the south. Adapting to these very diverse places, with such different climates and types of vegetation, led to the wren diversifying into at least twenty-seven different races, and maybe more – some of which are well on the way to turning into full species. So, if you want to see evolution in action, take a close look at wrens.

*

The combination of the wren's small size, distinctive appearance, and sheer ubiquity, has over the centuries led to many other, unrelated species, around the world as well as here in Britain, being christened 'wrens'.

Turn to any bird book written before the early twentieth century – from Gilbert White's *The Natural History of Selborne*, published in 1789, through the nineteenth-century works of Thomas Bewick, George Montagu, William Yarrell and William MacGillivray, all the way to Thomas Coward, writing in the 1920s – and you'll find references to the 'golden-crested wren' and, even more confusingly, to three different species of 'willow-wrens'.

To the modern reader, these may appear puzzling; until, that is, we realise that 'golden-crested wren' refers to the goldcrest, whose small size and rapid movements could easily have led our ancestors to conclude that it was related to the wren.

Likewise, the three 'willow-wrens' – the willow warbler, wood warbler and chiffchaff, often known as 'leaf-warblers' – also behave superficially like wrens when foraging for food. They do, however, look very different, being slender and olive-green or yellow in shade, rather than plump and brown.

These archaic names had more or less vanished by the time I was becoming interested in birds, during the 1960s and 1970s. But later on, when I began to travel outside Europe, I was surprised to discover how many birds, from families often quite unrelated to the wren, nevertheless bear its name.

In South and Central America, while there are wood-wrens and nightingale-wrens – which are fully paid-up members of the wren family – we also find the wren-like rushbird, and no fewer than 65 different species of antwren, which are not. Like our wren, though, they are rapid and furtive when foraging, and often pose with their tail cocked up behind their back. So it's easy to see why they were given the name.

Africa, too, can claim a quartet of birds with 'wren' in their names: the four wren-warblers, whose cocked tails, barred underparts and long, slender bills do lend them a superficial similarity with genuine wrens. The Asian wren-babblers share those same features, as does the North American wrentit, found in a narrow strip of land along the Pacific coast.

Australia is surely the world champion at naming birds because they look vaguely like wrens, with almost fifty different species bearing the name. As with our familiar robin redbreast, whose name was attached by homesick British colonists to any perky little bird with a red (or even pink or yellow) breast, so the first settlers of Australia dubbed any bird they came across which had a cocked tail a 'wren'.

Thus there are grasswrens, heathwrens, fieldwrens, scrubwrens, emu-wrens and a single species of fernwren, confined to tropical North Queensland. Most are small and slender, and come in various shades of grey and brown, rather like our own familiar species.

Not so the fairy-wrens, most of which sport a wondrous variety of dazzling shades of blue, and carry equally impressive names, including variegated, lovely, splendid and superb. In 2013, the superb fairy-wren was voted Australia's favourite bird, narrowly edging another familiar species, the Australian magpie (also unrelated to our bird of that name), into second place.

Finally, there is the sad story of the Stephens Island wren, a tiny, flightless bird found only on its eponymous home, off the South Island of New Zealand. This bird's main claim to fame is that, soon after a new lighthouse-keeper brought his cat Tibbles to the island in early 1894, the

Stephens Island wren vanished. As an editorial in *The Press* (a Christchurch-based newspaper) reported barely a year later, in March 1895, 'There is very good reason to believe that the bird is no longer to be found on the island, and, as it is not known to exist anywhere else, it has apparently become quite extinct.'

All these many species that include the word 'wren' in their name are a testimony to the power of this little bird in the minds of our ancestors. In his 1529 poem 'The Book of Phillip Sparrow', John Skelton wrote of 'The pretty wren, that is Our Lady's hen' (the first recorded reference to the wren in its current spelling). Yet he could surely never have imagined that, almost five centuries later, that name would have spread to all four corners of the world, and be bestowed on such a wide range of birds – whose only shared characteristics are their small size, active feeding habits and, most of all, that famous cocked tail.

FEBRUARY

This Bird, in my opinion, is a pretty, sweet, dapper Songster, being of a Nature cheerful; as he is pleasant to the Ear, so he is to the Eye; and when he sings cocks up his Tail, and throws out his notes with so much alacrity and pleasure that I know not any Bird of its bigness more delights the sense of Hearing.

Nicholas Cox, 'Of the Wren',
The Gentleman's Recreation, c. 1686

The weather may be cold, damp and dull, and spring is still quite some time away, but the mornings and evenings are finally getting lighter, and there are the first signs that the countryside is coming back to life.

On a late-afternoon stroll around my Somerset village, I notice a few snowdrops in the churchyard, punching through the hard earth, and there are hazel and pussy willow catkins along the hedgerows in the lanes behind my home. A song thrush is singing its clear, repetitive song somewhere in the distance, while the syncopated sound of the great tit also echoes across the wintry landscape. After such a long winter, these early hints of change produce a welcome spring in my step.

And then I hear it: the loud, strident and assertive song of a cock wren, singing his heart out to all within earshot. As a herald of spring, this little bird takes quite some beating.

Of course, he isn't singing this striking song for my benefit – nor for any other human or avian ear; apart, that is, from his fellow wrens. For like all the world's 5,000 or so species of songbird – including sparrows and starlings, thrushes and warblers, finches and buntings, and many more – he is sending out a loud, clear and unequivocal message, but only to members of his own kind.

To his fellow males, he is asserting control over his territory, by warning them to keep their distance. But to any listening females, the very same notes contain a much more conciliatory, even romantic, message: 'Would you consider pairing up with me, settling down and raising a family?' There might be a very long way to go before his brood of chicks successfully fledge and leave their nest, some time in May or June, but this loud, high-pitched – and utterly unignorable – song clearly signals the onset of the reproductive process.

People are often surprised at the incredibly high volume of the wren's song. Of all Britain's songbirds, it is the second loudest, after Cetti's warbler, and the loudest for a bird of its small size – it is said to be proportionately ten times as powerful as the crow of a cockerel.

The poet John Clare, writing in the early nineteenth century in rural Northamptonshire, noted that 'Its song is more loud than the Robin's and very pleasant, though it is uttered in broken raptures by sudden starts and endings. . .'

Why wrens sing quite so loudly is still a puzzle. One theory is they need to outcompete their rivals because their population density is so high, and territories are as a consequence tightly packed together, especially in gardens. But that is surely also true for robins, blackbirds and song thrushes, none of which seems to feel the need to turn the volume up to eleven.

Some bird books suggest, quite wrongly, that the wren's rich and varied cornucopia of notes and phrases always ends with a trill. In fact, this distinctive phrase has been more aptly described by Dominic Couzens as 'the twiddle in the middle', as it generally occurs roughly halfway through the wren's song, rather than at the climax.

In another analogy, he likens the wren to an opera singer giving her all before the final curtain falls. But there's one crucial difference: the male wren must continue to produce his song time and again, for weeks or even months on end.

Wrens are very territorial, and males will often start singing before Christmas if conditions are mild. But whatever the weather, soon after New Year – either at the end of January or the start of February, depending on where you are in the country – you will hear that familiar and distinctive song. Yet I was still pleasantly surprised when I heard this bird: my first singing wren of the year.

Not that they need mild weather to make them burst into song. A few years ago, when heavy snow fell across much of southern England in the middle of January, I went for a walk around our parish. In the broad hawthorn hedgerow behind our home I heard two wrens going hammer-and-tongs at one another, in a whited-out landscape in which no other bird – not even a robin – was making a sound.

In sharp contrast, on mild late winter days, when the first buff-tailed bumblebees and brimstone butterflies are emerging from their winter hiding places in the woodshed, the rousing chorus of wrens in our garden really does make it seem as if spring is just around the corner.

As Edward Armstrong himself noted, the wren's song, while undeniably striking, is considered by many people to be somewhat unmusical. He did, however, suggest that 'It impresses the listener as cheerful,' and also noted that the Breton name for the wren translates as 'the cheerful one'.

But even the wren's greatest fans would probably admit that its song lacks the purity and melodiousness of our most popular songsters, such as the robin and blackbird, or my personal favourite, the song thrush.

It is also unable to match the two birds most favoured by the poets, the skylark and the nightingale.

In his book *Birdscapes*, Jeremy Mynott draws our attention to a now long-forgotten work by Stanley Morris, published in 1924, entitled *Bird-Song*. In an appendix, Morris published a 'league table' of what he considered to be the 'best' songsters, assessed in five categories: Mellowness of tone, Sprightly notes, Plaintive notes, Compass and Execution. Each category earned a maximum of 20 marks, giving a possible total of 100.

Not surprisingly, the nightingale was way out in front, with 90 marks, followed by the linnet (74), blackcap (66), skylark (63) and the 'titlark' – either the tree or meadow pipit – with 60. The usual favourites – the robin, thrush and blackbird, were way down the list; as was the wren, which scored just 20 – 12 of which were for 'Sprightly notes' – with a big fat zero for both 'Mellowness of tone' and 'Plaintive notes'. As Mynott wryly points out, this scoring system appears to be rather fallible, especially as the wren gets just 4 out of 20 marks for 'Execution', hardly a fitting tribute to the energy it expends while singing.

Yet like Nicholas Cox, whose praise of the wren's sweet and cheerful sound appears at the head of this chapter, many early ornithologists rated the wren's sound rather more highly than Stanley Morris. The nineteenth-century ornithologist George Montagu thought that the wren 'enlivens the rustic garden with its song', while William Yarrell, writing in the 1840s, praised its 'shrill and lively strain'. His contemporary William MacGillivray, a Scotsman of an altogether dourer character, nevertheless praised the wren for its 'pleasing, full, rich and mellow song'.

W. H. Hudson was even more effusive:

His song is his greatest charm. It is unlike that of any other British melodist – a loud, bright lyric, the fine, clear, high-pitched notes and trills issuing in a continuous rapid stream from beginning to end. Although rapid, and ending somewhat abruptly, it is a beautiful and finished performance, in which every note is distinctly enunciated and has its value.

As Hudson also observed, the wren's song may be surprisingly loud, but it does not carry as far as the sound of other birds: 'the notes of the song-thrush, blackbird, and nightingale can be heard at nearly three times the distance.' Even so, in calm weather a singing wren can be heard within a range of 600 yards, while the St Kilda wren is said to be audible from over half a mile away.

For me, the most evocative description of the wren's song comes from the essayist and Irish nationalist Robert Wilson Lynd, who in 1922 wrote:

It is a song as brilliant as a rainbow in a wet sky – brilliant as a dance of rainbows. There is a shameless optimism in it that clothes the bare hedges with something better than leaves. There is no other resident bird so incapable of melancholy. The robin is often pensive, and sings to us . . . as though he sympathised with us. But the wren never sings except to say that it is the best of all possible worlds.

True to his methodical character, Edward Armstrong examined the exact nature of the wren's song in less poetic, and more forensic, detail. He was aided by transcriptions from Miss Gladys Page-Wood, a pioneer in the analysis of birdsong using musical terms.

They revealed that the song of the wren is higher in pitch than almost any other British bird: only the shimmering song of the wood warbler, and the mechanical reeling of the grasshopper warbler, register at a higher frequency. Page-Wood compared the wren to the top note on the piano, which at about 4,100 kilohertz is quite high-pitched.

Armstrong also noted that a typical wren's song consists of distinct phrases, each lasting five or six seconds, and punctuated with a pause between, so that normally he sings about five or six separate phrases every minute. Each phrase consists of what sounds like between thirty and fifty different notes; though by recording a wren's song, and slowing it down to a pitch and rate more accessible to the human ear, scientists have discovered that each phrase may consist of as many as 130 different notes.

Let's do the math, as our American cousins might say. If a typical wren sings five phrases of, say, 100 notes every minute, that makes 500 notes per minute, or 30,000 notes per hour. Making a conservative assumption that a wren sings for three or four hours every day, that comes to roughly 100,000 notes every twenty-four hours.

In fact, most wrens sing for far longer each day. As a young man, the zoologist R. B. (Bob) Clark published a statistical analysis of the wren's song in the magazine *British Birds*. He noted that, in line with many other songbirds, wrens usually began to sing about thirty to forty minutes before sunrise, and then continued to do so at more or less the same frequency for another five or six hours, following which they still sang from time to time. He also found that they continued to sing well into June, at least four months after they had begun.

So, given that a wren may sing for 120 days a year, this would suggest that its annual output is somewhere close to twelve million notes. Quite an accomplishment for any bird – let alone one so small.

Nor is the wren's song always exactly the same, even though to our untrained ear it might seem so. Armstrong claimed to be able to detect a growing sense of urgency when a singing male is confronted by a rival – what he called its 'fighting song': 'His normal song becomes rapid, abbreviated and congested – much as when two frenzied people quarrel they utter a stream of incoherent insults at each other.'

Armstrong went on to observe that in most circumstances – though not always – this more aggressive outburst is enough to repel any intruding male. He also discovered that when two cock wrens do sing together – in a 'sing-off', familiar to viewers of TV talent contests – one bird will attempt to alternate his song over that of his rival, a choral technique known as 'antiphonal singing'. This, he suggested, enabled each bird to hear the other's song, which would not be possible if they sang at the same time as one another.

In his popular book *The Charm of Birds*, first published in 1927, Britain's longest-serving foreign secretary, Sir Edward Grey, recalled that he once watched a wren singing inside a greenhouse to a rival on the outside:

> I watched it for some time at a distance of not more than two or three feet, perhaps even less. . . The attitude of my wren when listening was intent and still; when it replied the animation and vehemence were such that it seemed as if this little atom of life might be shattered by its own energy.

Once a resident male wren has established his territory, and fought off any potential rivals, his next task is to find a mate. And if the amount of energy he expends on his song is impressive, then so are his efforts at courtship. Described by Armstrong as 'very beautiful', it is also – on the male's part at least – extremely hard work.

Once again, he modifies his song, making it slower and more melodious in tone, as if he recognises the need to switch from the mood of aggression to one of persuasion. This 'gentle warbling', as Armstrong described it, may go on for longer than the usual song-phrase: up to half a minute at times, so that it can be 'heard to full perfection' by his intended mate.

From this time of year onwards, throughout the early part of spring, I sometimes see one wren in hot pursuit of another, flying rapidly around our garden or along the nearby hedgerow. Given that male and female wrens look identical, it would be easy to assume that this is an established male, who already has possession of a breeding territory, seeing off a rival.

Usually, though, that is not what is actually happening. The pursuing bird is indeed the incumbent male; but the one being chased is a female.

Armstrong, who had the advantage over me of having placed coloured rings on the birds in his study area, and so could tell which sex was which, described this pursuit in great detail:

> Especially during the morning hours one may often catch glimpses of the two tiny birds speeding from bush to bush, the cock always in the rear. When the brief chase ends he may warble sweetly as he moves from twig to twig above the herbage in which the female has taken refuge, or he may go off through his territory singing and feeding.

Armstrong also observed that, at the end of some chases, the male would 'pounce' on the female; not necessarily mating, but to stimulate her to become more receptive to copulation, which would then happen later on. The cock may also sit above her and quiver his wings, as described in this delightful extract from Armstrong's notebook:

> Wren displaying on branch with tremulous, widespread, nearly level wings and beautifully fanned tail, uttering somewhat subdued, excited and abbreviated song. He flies close to the ivy-twined trunk where the female is lurking. Shortly afterwards I hear a grating call. His wingbeats as he flew were rather slow; possibly also his wings were not fully spread. The sun shone luminously through them.

As with most courtship displays in nature – whether mostly visual, like that of the peacock, or aural, as in songbirds such as the wren – the male seems to be putting in all the effort, while his intended mate more or less ignores him. But compared to what will happen next, during the month of March, the song is the easy bit.

The female is not always the passive partner: sometimes she will actively solicit the male for sex. She will at first fly away, but then allow herself to be caught (as Armstrong describes it) like Virgil's nymph, who 'runs off to the willows – and hopes I saw her first'. Just like the antics of boxing hares, this is her way of testing not just his ardour and his enthusiasm for her, but also his overall health and fitness, before she consents to mate.

Wrens have not always been Britain's commonest bird. When I was growing up, during the 1960s and 1970s, most bird books put the blackbird and the chaffinch in the top two of the 'league table' of most numerous species, with the wren perhaps fourth or fifth. Earlier still, the wren was even lower down the rankings. Writing in 1951, Max Nicholson could confidently assert that:

> Although perhaps the most widespread bird in the British Isles . . . the wren is undoubtedly far outnumbered in total by such species as the chaffinch and the blackbird, and after a severe winter is so reduced that it must fall well below the first dozen species in order of abundance.

But we should remember that Nicholson was writing soon after two of the worst winters of the twentieth century – the long, hard winters of 1940/41 and 1946/47 – following which the wren population would indeed have been considerably reduced.

Another incredibly harsh winter – the infamous 'Big Freeze' of

1962/63 – would soon occur, so it's perhaps hardly surprising that when I was young the wren certainly didn't appear to be very common. This was not helped by the fact that as a child I was not particularly observant, and so undoubtedly overlooked wrens in favour of the showier chaffinches, blackbirds, robins and house sparrows in and around our garden.

I can still recall the publication, in 1976, of the first BTO *Atlas of Breeding Birds in Britain and Ireland*. This seminal work provided, for the very first time, a really detailed distribution map for each of 220 or so breeding species, based on a comprehensive nationwide survey of 3,862 10-km-x-10-km squares.

In terms of ubiquity, the wren came second only to the skylark, occupying no fewer than 97 per cent of the squares. The unnamed author of the text on the wren noted that although the species is 'severely affected by very cold weather . . . there had been unusually mild winters in the five years leading up to and also during the Atlas period'. Given that the survey took place only a few years after that terrible winter of 1962/63, which reduced Britain's wren numbers by up to 90 per cent, we might assume that they were being rather optimistic about the wren's powers of recovery.

However, an accompanying graph, which used data from another BTO survey, the Common Birds Census, revealed that although wren numbers on farmland and woodland had indeed plummeted to below half their baseline population following the 1962/63 winter, just three years later the population had indeed recovered; and by 1974, it was well above the baseline index.

The author also pointed out that the hundred or so 10-km squares where wrens were not recorded were mostly remote coastal or mountainous areas. Locating a bird as small and unobtrusive as the wren during a short survey period might have been difficult, so that 'there must be a suspicion that sometimes they were overlooked.' Given this caveat, it seems highly likely that the wren was actually Britain's most abundant bird at the time.

The 1993 BTO *Atlas*, for which the field research took place two decades later between 1988 and 1991, showed the changes that had occurred for each species since the previous survey. The wren's abundance was virtually unchanged: it bred in 3,748 10-km squares, just seven fewer than in 1968–72.

The 1993 *Atlas* also showed, for the very first time, the relative abundance of each species by means of coloured maps. These revealed that the wren was most numerous south of a line between the River Mersey and River Humber – the southern third of Britain – with population density clearly rising towards the south and west. Farther north, and especially in the uplands, wrens were spread far more thinly.

In 1986 the BTO had produced the first (and, so far, only) dedicated *Winter Atlas*, based on three seasons' fieldwork carried out from 1981 to 1982 and from 1983 to 1984. Even in the depths of winter, the wren was only missing from the very highest and bleakest upland areas: parts of north and west Wales, the uplands of northern England and the Scottish Highlands.

The author of the account, John Marchant, did note that because wrens are so tiny and light in weight, they are less able to store fat than larger birds, and so chill more rapidly. Because of this, they are very vulnerable to a sudden drop in temperature, especially when this prevents them from finding food. However, he also observed that wrens actually cope quite well with snowy conditions, by adopting a behaviour more

akin to a small mammal than any bird: 'By its ability to feed beneath snow cover in winter, this species, to a degree, lives up to its scientific name and becomes at least partly "subterranean".'

Acknowledging the volatility of wren numbers, due to the difference in mortality between cold and mild winters, Marchant estimated that during the winters surveyed there had been between twelve and twenty million individual wrens in Britain and Ireland, confirming its position as one of our commonest birds.

By the time of the most recent nationwide survey, the *Bird Atlas* 2007–11 (published in 2013), technology had moved on hugely, allowing really detailed analysis of the records. This *Atlas* provided data from both the key seasons of the year, with the breeding and wintering range and numbers presented together for the very first time.

As in previous *Atlases*, the ubiquity of the wren was obvious – the species was recorded in at least 97 per cent of 10-km squares all year round. As the authors pointed out, with so few areas unoccupied (and most of these currently unsuitable – though climate change may ultimately change this) there was little scope for the wren to make any further advances.

But there was still room for numbers to increase where wrens were already present, and for the first time this *Atlas* revealed that the species' population density had increased considerably in areas towards the north and west of the wren's range, such as northern Scotland and Ireland. Indeed, in Scotland as a whole, breeding numbers were up by almost a third.

The success of the wren was put in perspective by a paper published in *British Birds* in February 2013. Entitled 'Population Estimates of Birds in Great Britain and the United Kingdom', it made a valiant attempt to produce detailed numbers of total breeding pairs, not just for each species, but for Britain's bird population as a whole.

Two headline figures, in particular, struck me. First, that of an estimated 84 million pairs of birds, the top ten species accounted for almost 60 per cent of the total. And second, that the wren alone – so often overlooked and ignored by most people – accounted for one in ten of all Britain's breeding birds.

For such a humble and unassuming creature, that is quite an achievement.

MARCH

The ouzel cock, so black of hue

With orange-tawny bill,

The throstle with his note so true,

The wren with little quill. . .

William Shakespeare, *A Midsummer*
Night's Dream, Act III, Scene 1

March may come in like a lion, and go out like a lamb, at least according to weather folklore. But with the onset of global climate change, and its increasingly noticeable effects on the already unpredictable British weather, this has become a tricky month for many wild creatures.

In some years, temperatures across much of Britain can plummet towards zero, with late falls of snow. In others, the mercury may surge into the late teens or even low twenties, bringing clear, warm and sunny days, more like late spring or early summer than March. As a result, the onset of the seasons is becoming far less predictable too, with spring sometimes arriving very early, and sometimes much later than usual.

This topsy-turvy weather affects birds such as the wren in two ways. First – and above all else – they need to survive until the end of the winter. This is a time when natural food resources are at their lowest, and the birds' energy levels and body weight may also be falling. Yet they also need to find enough energy to begin the process of breeding. This is the first lap in the long and arduous race to reproduce, in which, as time goes on, those left behind at the starting line may struggle to keep up with the leaders.

When it comes to breeding wrens are, like many resident species, reasonably early starters. They do not begin as soon as larger species such as the blackbird or song thrush, which may already have built a nest and laid eggs by February, especially if the winter has been exceptionally mild. But nor do they start nesting as late as the returning summer migrants which, having flown back from Africa and arrived in April or early May, will not begin to breed until spring is well underway.

Unlike the fickle British weather, another factor in the timing of breeding is completely predictable. The arrival of the Spring Equinox, on or around 20 March each year, signals the moment when – everywhere across the globe – daylight and night-time hours are more or less equal.

From then on, in Britain as across the rest of the middle regions of the northern hemisphere, the balance begins to shift. We turn from the long, dark nights of winter to the short ones of summer, with all the joy that brings. That is why, despite the Met Office's decision to base the four seasons on the calendar months of the year (so that spring runs from 1 March to 31 May), I prefer to use the shifts of the Earth – the spring and autumn equinoxes, and the summer and winter solstices – to mark their changing.

Now, barely a week into March, there are still few signs that spring is about to kick off. Apart from those snowdrops in the village churchyard, and crocuses of various colours (and dubious provenance) along the roadside verges, it might as well still be winter – whatever the Met Office says.

Robins and song thrushes are singing lustily – as they have been since virtually the start of the year. And unseen, in the middle of a broad green churchyard yew, I can hear the thin, high-pitched sound of a goldcrest, accompanied by the syncopated see-saw song of a coal tit. But easterly winds, only occasionally punctuated by spells of wet and stormy weather from the west, have made this a miserable start to the month. I have to force myself to go out and look for birds.

I'm not the only organism responding to the promise of spring, brought about by earlier sunrises and later sunsets. Impelled by the increase in daylight hours, a male wren has also decided to kick-start his breeding season by moving on to the next stage after song and courtship: nest building. Yet he does so in rather an unusual – and for a British bird, unique – way.

Most songbirds, including the familiar robin, song thrush and blackbird, build a classic, cup-shaped nest out of grass, which they then line with moss, leaves, feathers or mud. Others, such as the nuthatch and members of the tit family, choose to make their nests in holes in trees (or in nest boxes), giving them a degree of protection that the others lack. But only a few species – including the house martin, long-tailed tit, magpie and dipper – build a domed, ball-shaped nest like that of the wren.

The wren's unusual nest was described almost 500 years ago by the sixteenth-century ornithologist, cleric and radical William Turner. Turner was the first Englishman to update the classical observations of Aristotle and Pliny, which had held sway for almost two millennia, by testing them against reality.

Turner's translation of Aristotle's detailed description of the form, materials and structure of the wren's nest is a testament to the acuteness of the Greek philosopher's field observation skills:

The nest is outwardly of moss and inwardly of feathers, wool or down, but mainly of feathers. The nest has the form of an upright egg standing on one of its ends, while in the middle of one side there is a little postern, as it were, by which the bird goes in and out.

The poet William Wordsworth also used close observation of a wren's nest in his poem 'Contrast', in which he examined the differences between the showy parrot and the subtler wren:

> This moss-lined shed, green, soft, and dry,
> Harbours a self-contented Wren,
> Not shunning man's abode, though shy,
> Almost as thought itself, of human ken.

A domed, enclosed, egg-shaped nest has two major advantages. First, it keeps the eggs and chicks warm and sheltered, which may be crucial to their survival if a cold spell brings lower temperatures, or during a heavy fall of rain or snow. Second, and even more importantly, it renders the contents of the nest less visible to any passing predator, and so far less likely to be raided.

The reason why wrens build a domed nest in the first place is a legacy of their evolutionary origins. Long before they began to spread north, and eventually moved into Asia and Europe, our wren's ancestors evolved in the tropical regions of Central America. Here, their nests needed to be enclosed to deter the much larger range of predators, including snakes. But a domed nest also provided a fortuitously beneficial side-effect: added warmth. This may be the key factor that allowed the Eurasian wren to spread so successfully across the temperate regions of its new home, eventually reaching even beyond the Arctic Circle.

In normal circumstances, when nesting in a garden or a wood, the wren makes its nest out of leaves and moss, hidden inside some kind of natural cavity such as a fallen or hollow tree trunk, or behind a curtain of ivy. In other habitats, where the availability of nest sites and materials can vary, wrens will nest inside gaps in drystone walls, or in other narrow clefts or crevices. That is especially true of the various island races.

Wrens are, more than any other birds apart from the swallow and barn owl, also inclined to nest inside buildings, where they perhaps feel safer from predators. John Clare was familiar with this habit, indeed considered it the norm, as he described in one of his *Natural History Letters*: '[It] builds its nest mostly in the roof of hovels and under the eaves of sheds about the habitations of man though it is often found in the cowsheds. . .'

Whatever the setting, however, most wrens' nests are fairly low: usually only a few feet above the ground, though they have been recorded at heights of up to seven metres in a tall tree.

As George Montagu noted, the wren also has the crucial ability to

Pl. 705.

2

adapt the materials he uses to make his nest to suit the surroundings, and what may be readily available. 'If built against the side of a hayrick, it is composed of hay; if against the side of a tree covered with white moss, it is made of that material; and with green moss if against a tree covered with the same, or in a bank.'

Conversely, Thomas Coward pointed out that while wrens' nests are indeed often very well concealed, thanks to their choice of suitable material, such as 'grass in a haystack, moss on a rock, lichens in a tree, leaves amongst litter', others are 'suicidally conspicuous'.

While wrens do not quite rival robins for their bizarre choice of nest sites, they have been known to build their nest in a bicycle bag hanging up in a shed, in an item of clothing as it dries on a washing-line, amongst a wreath, in a scarecrow's pocket, and even inside a human skull.

The nature writer and photographer Polly Pullar recalls that many years ago, when she worked with Highland ponies in the small town of Auchterarder, near the famous Gleneagles Hotel, she would regularly take them to a blacksmith's forge in nearby Tullibardine.

The old blacksmith there was one Jimmy Aitken, and he had horseshoes arranged in sizes and hung all around the stone walls. One year, one of the nests had been made around a hook of horseshoes. It was quite close to the forge and yet the sparks did not deter the female from raising no fewer than nine chicks. Old Jimmy was very amused, saying that the shoes she had chosen were naturally one of the most popular sizes, and so he had to make a whole lot more to replace them until after nesting was finished. For some weeks afterwards, the place was alive with hungry baby wrens!

But perhaps the strangest location for a wren's nest, which Thomas Coward saw for himself preserved in Chester Museum, was a nest 'tucked between the limp wing and dry carcase of a Sparrow-Hawk hanging on a keeper's gibbet'.

There is also a famous legend about the seventh-century holy man St Malo of Brittany, and his encounter with a nesting wren:

One day he was busy with the brethren in the vineyard, pruning the vines, and for better speed in his work took off his cloak and laid it out of sight. When his work was done and he came to take his cloak, he found that the small bird whom common folk call a wren had laid an egg on it. And knowing that God's care is not far from the birds, since not one of them falls on the ground without the Father, he let his cloak lie there, till the eggs were hatched and the wren brought out her brood.

One clever trick up the wren's sleeve is that the nest is usually built during or just after a fall of rain, so that the material used is damp; that way, when the weather clears up, the nest 'shrinks to fit', making it stronger and more resilient. Wrens have even been reported as dipping their nesting material into water to soak it. This may explain why wrens do so well in the relatively damp climate of south-west Britain and Ireland.

Once the nest is more or less built, the threshold of the entrance hole is then reinforced with dried stems of grass. These provide added strength: crucial when the male and female are feeding the chicks, as they will be going in and out of the nest many hundreds of times in a single day.

★

The other major difference between wrens and most other songbirds is that instead of the female building the nest, that duty falls on the male. And here's the twist: he doesn't just build one nest, but several – usually five or six, but up to twelve in a single breeding season.

Known as 'cock's nests', these are part of a grand strategy on the part of the male wren. They take an awful lot of work: each morning, he wakes before dawn and begins to sing, often for up to two hours. Then, as soon as it becomes light enough for him to see what he is doing, he begins to fetch material and starts to build each nest.

This is quite a task, as George Montagu observed: 'It is a . . . curious sight to see a wren carrying a piece of moss almost as large as its own body.' Montagu also noticed that typically the male uses a well-thought-out method of construction. 'It first sketches an oval outline of the structure by gluing, with saliva, bits of moss all round . . . so as to be narrower at top than at bottom.' The cock wren then goes on to add more pieces of moss until he has made 'a large hemisphere . . . about twenty times the bulk of the little architect. . .'

The dimensions of a typical nest are roughly 11 x 13 x 14.5 cm (about 4 x 5 x 6 inches) – the equivalent of a human being building a structure two to three metres (seven to ten feet) in diameter. And remember, he needs to make up to twelve of these in a single breeding season.

While all this is going on, he can't afford to neglect his other duties, such as defending his newly won territory against any passing males. Thus, every twenty minutes or so, he stops his work and utters a few bursts of song, patrolling the borders of his territory to check for rivals, before heading off to find food to keep up his energy levels. This continues throughout much of the day, though nest-building activity does tend to tail off in the afternoons.

The male wren will continue to build his series of nests for several weeks – even on occasion months – adding the odd leaf with a house-proud flourish, before he is finally ready to show off his handiwork to his mate.

Ironically, the vast majority of these nests will remain unused. But there is still a method behind his apparent madness. Having built the nests, the cock then does a kind of 'estate agent's tour' with a female in tow. She looks each nest up and down, paying particular attention to both the quality of the build and the site the male has chosen, and only then makes her decision. Usually she will choose the most well-hidden nest, minimising the chances of her eggs or chicks being taken by predators.

To encourage her to make her final choice, as the male reaches each nest on his circuit he starts to sing. Then, if she seems encouraged by his efforts, he may even hop right inside and continue to sing from within.

Dominic Couzens has likened the male wren to a property developer, 'buying' portions of land on which he builds his nests, in the hope that more females will move in and breed with him. By investing all that effort, he will be rewarded by producing as many young as possible, thereby passing on his genetic heritage down the generations, even if by then he is long gone.

Wrens, like other songbirds, sometimes also use props in their displays. At this time of year, what could be more natural than for the male wren to pick up a piece of nesting material and, instead of incorporating it into the nest structure immediately, use it as part of his continued attempts at courtship? Just as great crested grebes use water-weed in their famous 'penguin dance', so a male wren will sometimes wave a piece of

moss or a leaf at his mate, while quivering his wings and calling.

When he thinks that he has aroused the hen's interest in a particular nest, the cock wren will often up the ante by using a very specific form of the quivering wing display, in order to guide her towards the nest. Armstrong called this the 'nest-invitation display', observing that the male usually begins at some distance from the actual nest, luring the female along by a combination of sounds and actions, as she lurks deep inside the undergrowth.

As she gets nearer and nearer the nest itself, he becomes more and more animated, until he stops outside and spreads his tail, droops his (still-quivering) wings, and invites her to come in and take a look. At first, she seems reluctant, and may even begin to forage for tiny insects or spiders.

This is a classic example of what scientists call 'displacement activity', in which, during a highly tense moment in the courtship process, one or both of the pair breaks off to indulge in feeding or preening, feigning apparent indifference. Undaunted, he tries again, 'singing his soft and slender song while holding his wings like a tremulous cloak about him'.

Then, unable to contain his excitement any longer, he darts inside the nest, waits a few moments, and then emerges – as if showing her that all is safe. This is the moment of truth and it usually works. The female enters the nest for the very first time; a nest that will be her home for the next few weeks – the most crucial period of her short but eventful life.

She has given him the sign that he has been waiting for: finally, she is happy with this particular property. Having made her choice, she will then spend a day or two organising the interior furnishings, bringing back hundreds of tiny feathers in order to create a soft bed, onto which she will lay her eggs. On one occasion, this process took as long as a week, but perhaps that particular female was especially house-proud.

Building so many nests seems like a lot of unnecessary hard work for the male, but again there is a logic to his extra efforts. Having persuaded one female to pair up with him, and begin nesting, he then repeats the process all over again. For, again unlike most songbirds, wrens are polygynous, with a single male often mating with two, or even three, females.

This behaviour is, however, much more frequent in more forgiving, temperate latitudes. That's because in places with warmer spring weather the growing season is longer, which in turn means there is more food for the incubating female and – when they hatch – her chicks. To-

Wren nesting in an old coat's pocket

wards the northern fringes of the wren's range, or on offshore islands, where the weather tends to be harsher and there is less food, wrens are usually monogamous, as it takes all the efforts of both cock and hen to raise a single brood.

The domed nest provides another major advantage here: because the chicks are hidden away, and there is plenty of available food close to most nests, the male does not take much part in the raising of the chicks, leaving this task almost totally to the female. So all that effort on his part early in the season does prove, eventually, worthwhile.

Edward Armstrong came to believe that it was this flexibility in the wren's behaviour – constantly being able to adapt its lifestyle to suit its surroundings – that has been the key to the species' huge success. It's perhaps unlikely that he ever revealed the wren's unorthodox sexual shenanigans to his parishioners – but he was broad-minded enough to see the many advantages that polygyny conveyed on the wren.

1. Common Bunting.   2. Black-headed Bunting.   3. Yellow-hammer.   4. Cirl Bunting.   5. Chaffinch.
6. Tree Sparrow.   7. House Sparrow.   8. Greenfinch.   9. Hawfinch.   10. Goldfinch.   11. Linnet.
12. Redpole.   13. Twite.   14. Bullfinch.   15. Crossbill.   16. Creeper.   17. Wren.   18. Nuthatch.
19. Cuckoo.   20. Swallow.

APRIL

I believe a leaf of grass is no less than the journeywork of
the stars,
And the pismire is equally perfect, and a grain of sand, and
the egg of the wren. . .

Walt Whitman, 'Song of Myself',
Leaves of Grass, 1891

On this early Easter weekend, as March winds shift gently into April showers, spring has finally arrived in my little corner of the West Country. In our garden, chiffchaffs persistently call out their name, and robins sing from the hawthorn bushes; meanwhile, green woodpeckers laugh loudly, but unseen, from the adjacent orchard.

The most obvious sign of spring is, of course, the much-awaited arrival of the swallows, which have flown all the way here from their winter quarters in southern Africa, to nest in the barn next to my home. One pair seem to be celebrating their return, as they fly high up into the Somerset sky, twittering to one another in the initial stages of courtship, before swooping back down into the barn where they will soon build their nest.

For the more modest (and considerably less visible) wrens, this part of the reproductive process is long since over. It has been hard work getting so far. Now, having survived the winter, warded off any rivals, attracted a mate, and chosen a place to nest, they are ready for the next stage in their breeding season.

Having mated with the male, after a period of five or six days has elapsed, the female wren will finally begin producing her eggs. Wrens usually lay five or six eggs, though sometimes they produce as many as eight or nine. 'Look where the youngest wren of nine comes,' announces Sir Toby Belch in Shakespeare's *Twelfth Night* but, as Edward Armstrong suggests, this may have been an exaggeration on the part of the playwright.

The Victorian ornithologist William MacGillivray wrote of two specific instances where far more eggs than usual were discovered inside a single wren's nest. Both were in Scotland, and both were reported to him by the same gentleman: a mysterious 'Mr Weir', whose eyewitness account is reproduced verbatim by MacGillivray:

> Robert Smith, weaver in Bathgate, told me, that a few years ago, he saw in a nest, which was built on the bank of a rivulet about two miles from Linlithgow, seventeen eggs; and James D. Baillie, Esq. informed me that in June last, he took out of one which he discovered in a spruce tree near Polkemmet House, sixteen eggs. He put them in again, and, on returning sometime afterwards, found them all hatched.

A traditional Scottish verse comparing the relative productivity of the wood pigeon and the wren suggests that the smaller bird can produce even more eggs:

> The big Cushie-doo, only lays two
> The wee Cuddy-wran, lays twenty-wan.

But as with other 'record clutches', claimed for birds as varied as blue tits and pheasants, these large numbers are almost certainly the result of two females laying their eggs in the same nest. If so, even John Clare was fooled: in his *Natural History Letters* he wrote that 'it lays as many as fifteen or sixteen white eggs very small and faintly spotted with pink spots. . .'

The number of eggs produced does, however, vary depending on geographic location. In the south of Europe – such as Sicily or the Balearic Islands – wrens often lay as few as four eggs, and rarely more than six. But farther north, the clutch size gradually increases: six or seven eggs are laid in Germany and Poland, while in Iceland, the Faroe Islands and Norway a typical clutch numbers seven or eight.

The theory behind this increase is that in these northerly latitudes, with almost twenty-four-hour sunlight during late spring and early summer, there is a glut of food, allowing the wrens to raise more young. What contradicts this, though, is that in the north most wrens are monogamous, suggesting it takes greater effort to rear a family there. Maybe this paradox can be reconciled by the fact that in the south wrens generally have two broods, but in the north they only have one, so it makes sense to have as many chicks as they can in that single breeding attempt, as they will not get another chance until next year.

As with other birds – including domestic chickens – wrens can be induced to lay more eggs by the simple (but rather cruel) expedient of removing a single egg from the clutch each day. One study from Northern Ireland carried out before the Second World War, when egg collecting was still rife, noted that 'Boys make this little bird lay eggs to a vast number, by taking them gradually from the nest.'

The standard British clutch of five or six eggs may not sound a great many. But just consider that, with each egg weighing about one-and-a-half grams, and the female weighing just nine or ten grams, a full clutch is close to her own body weight in eggs. That's equivalent to an average female human producing quintuplets or sextuplets weighing between 11.5 and 14 kilos – roughly 25 to 31 pounds – each.

The eggs themselves are, to our eyes, very tiny: just 16 mm long by 13 mm wide (0.6 by 0.5 inches), smaller than those of any British breeding bird apart from the goldcrest, firecrest and long-tailed tit. They are off-white in colour, with variable reddish-brown speckling, mostly at the larger, more rounded end.

In order to lay her eggs, the hen wren must be at the peak of her health and fitness. She produces them early in the morning – usually before eight o'clock – on each successive day, until her clutch is complete.

As with other small birds (but not raptors and owls, which start incubating as soon as they have laid their first egg), she will not begin to sit on the eggs until they have all been laid. This ensures that the chicks will all hatch out at roughly the same time. Just before she begins to incubate, the female often roosts inside the nest for the whole night, as if getting ready for the long stint ahead.

The female does all the incubating, sitting tight for much of the day and night, and only occasionally leaving to stretch her legs and wings, and to feed. During this period – which normally lasts between fourteen and sixteen days – she is almost entirely self-reliant for food. However, the male does regularly return to the nest, and may sing outside, perhaps adding a few pieces of moss or leaves to the already-complete structure.

Even once the eggs have all been laid, and the incubation period has begun, things can easily go wrong, with the fickle British spring weather usually to blame. Unusually low temperatures – especially if the thermometer drops below freezing point – or severe frosts may provoke a female wren to desert her nest.

During spells of very warm weather, the female will leave the nest more often, and for longer, than when conditions are cooler. This is because in warm weather the eggs do not lose heat so rapidly. The enclosed nature of the wren's nest also reduces the risk of her being absent as, unlike in the open nest of a robin or blackbird, the eggs remain hidden, even when she is away.

On rare occasions, a female wren will continue to sit on her clutch even though the eggs are infertile, and so will never hatch. The longest recorded period of such behaviour involved a hen sitting on her eggs for twenty-six days before finally giving up. In cases when a predator has stolen the eggs, a female wren may also continue to sit in the empty nest – the longest recorded spell being fifteen days.

But if all has gone well, then towards the end of a fortnight or so's incubation period, a strange sound begins to emit from the middle of the nest. A series of almost inaudible clicks: very faint to our ears, but easily detectable by the parents. The sound is being made by the tiny chicks, inside the unhatched eggs, and is a signal to the female that hatching is about to begin.

Even though she began incubating the eggs at the same time, they do not always hatch together. Indeed, usually the last chick appears a day or so after the first. This is yet another of the wren's adaptations for survival, as it allows the older chicks to get more to eat than the youngsters, so that during times when food is short at least one or two will survive.

But it's a tricky balancing act. If the last chick hatches out too long after the first, then the youngsters will not be able to fledge and leave the nest together. That will mean their parents must divide their time between looking after chicks in two different locations: inside and outside the nest.

*

Like all songbird chicks, when the baby wrens are born they are naked, blind and completely helpless: or, as Armstrong memorably described them, 'like squirming maggots with their relatively huge heads resting on the feather mattress at the bottom of the nest'. Their skin is pink, and their head and back are covered with a thin layer of grey down.

But the instinct to survive is incredibly powerful, even in the first few moments of life. Almost as soon as a chick has hatched, it finds the strength to lift up its head into a vertical position, and open its beak wide so that it can be fed. This reveals a bright yellow mouth, with paler yellow edges – a stimulus for the parents to bring back food, and easily visible even inside the dark interior of the nest.

THE WREN.

The first feed usually takes place less than an hour after the chicks have hatched. At this time, the female will also carry the broken eggshells some distance from the nest, so as not to give away its location to predators.

Once again, at this stage the male does not do much to help, as he may be busy courting and nest-building for his second or even third mate. Fewer than half of all male wrens help feed the chicks at all, and even if they do, not usually until they are a few days old.

Left to her own devices, the female goes busily back and forth, grabbing tiny insects with her long, pointed bill, and then flying back to the nest to feed her hungry brood. She also spends long periods simply sitting on the tiny chicks to keep them warm, especially during the first few days after hatching.

When the chicks are about four or five days old, the sanitation inside the nest begins to become a problem. From then onwards, the female will carry away their droppings in what is known as a faecal sac (memorably dubbed 'shrink-wrapped poo' by Bill Oddie) and dispose of them some distance away from the nest.

By now the baby wrens have already changed considerably in appearance: their downy feathers are growing fast, and the inside of their mouths has turned a paler, lemon-yellow colour. In Armstrong's vividly poetic image, their tiny beaks 'waver on the craning necks like wan alpine blossoms stirred by a sudden breeze'.

Every time the female returns to the nest with food, the chicks respond by uttering a thin, high-pitched, squeaking sound. They are still unable to see, though from about their seventh day of life their eyes finally begin to open. Having weighed just over one gram at hatching, they grow rapidly throughout their time in the nest, putting on roughly a gram a day until, after nine or ten days, they reach their full adult weight.

During the last three or four days before they leave the nest (usually between fifteen and eighteen days after they first hatched), a female wren may be bringing back items of food as many as 500 or even 600 times a day – roughly once every two minutes during daylight hours. The highest number of visits recorded by Armstrong was forty-three in a single hour, by a lone female, which worked out at one every eighty-three seconds. Wrens feed their young more often at the start and end of the day, with the lowest number of feeding visits in the early afternoon.

The need to find so much food, on such a regular and consistent basis, highlights the importance of choosing the right place to nest. The location needs to be not just safe from predators, but also within easy reach of plenty of food, such as a site near water where there are plenty of mosquitoes and insect larvae. Timing is also crucial: if the period when the young are in the nest coincides with a mass hatching of moth caterpillars nearby, then the female's burden will be that much lighter.

The type of food brought back to the nest also varies as the chicks get bigger. Early on, it is mainly small insects such as flies, mosquitoes and moth caterpillars; later, the adult may bring back larger items such as crane flies (daddy-long-legs) and spiders.

In one unusual instance, the scientist Julian Huxley witnessed a wren feeding its young on trout fry. The female, whose nest was inside an old mill at a trout farm in Gloucestershire, would fly down to perch on the rim of a trough containing the baby trout, grab one from the surface of the water, and then return to her nearby nest to feed her catch to the chicks.

By the time the young wrens are almost ready to leave the nest, the female no longer has to squeeze inside every time she brings back food; instead, her youngsters – which by now are almost as big as she is – will congregate at the entrance hole, jostling one another for the best position to receive whatever she brings back. When doing so, they often call loudly to attract her attention. This is something of a double-edged sword: it increases each individual chick's chances of getting food, but also puts them in greater danger from passing predators, such as domestic cats.

Not all male wrens are so casual in their indifference to their hungry brood. In more extreme habitats, such as bleak, windswept offshore islands or the Arctic tundra, the (usually monogamous) males take a far greater share of the feeding duties.

We have already seen how, because of the wren's small size and endearing habits, it is held in great affection, not just by birders but amongst the public as a whole. Yet it was still a surprise when, in 1937, the Royal Mint announced a radical break with tradition for a coin that dated back to the thirteenth century.

They had decided that the traditional Britannia design on the obverse of the farthing (whose name derives from the obsolete word 'fourthing', meaning a quarter) would be replaced by a wren. The logic behind this move was that our smallest coin should feature our smallest bird – clearly no one had told the Mint that the goldcrest is even smaller.

This break with tradition would ultimately prove surprisingly uncontroversial, though the genesis of the change did have a few teething troubles. The wren design was originally planned to appear in 1936, on the obverse of farthings issued during the reign of the new monarch Edward VIII.

The new king, who had succeeded his father George V in January of that year, was keen to modernise the rather stuffy image of the monarchy. As a first step, he expressed his wish to change the design of the whole of Britain's coinage, from the farthing all the way up to the half-crown (worth two shillings and sixpence, or 12.5p in today's money).

But with the Mint's advisers (including a young Kenneth Clark, later of the BBC's *Civilisation* fame) fearing that such a wholesale change would not prove popular with the general public, Edward was eventually forced to give up his plan. Oddly, though, the Royal Mint did then change two coins to non-heraldic designs, choosing a sailing ship (Sir Francis Drake's *Golden Hind*) for the halfpenny, and a wren for the farthing.

The wren design was created by Harold Wilson Parker, who later taught at Goldsmith's College in south-east London, where his wife Constance Howard set up the Department of Embroidery. Parker was remembered by his students as 'a very quiet, gentle little man' who encouraged them to view design 'in the round', not simply as a flat, two-dimensional image. And it is certainly true that the wren design appeals precisely because it captures the energy of the bird so well: it appears poised to fly off the coin at any moment.

However, it took some time for the committee at the Royal Mint to give their final approval to Parker's design. This delay meant that the small number of Edward VIII farthings that featured the wren never actually came into circulation.

On 11 December 1936, the King made his famous abdication broadcast on the BBC Home Service, renouncing his claim to the British throne. Edward had taken this unprecedented step so that he could marry the twice-divorced American Wallis Simpson, whom he acknowledged with these poignant words: 'You must believe me when I tell you that I have found it impossible to carry the heavy burden of responsibility, and to discharge my duties as King as I would wish to do, without the help and support of the woman I love.'

Faced with a choice between love and duty, Edward had decided to abdicate in favour of his younger brother Bertie, who immediately acceded to the throne as King George VI. So the first new farthings, manufactured in bronze, and carrying the new monarch's image on one side and a portrait of a perky, cock-tailed wren on the other, appeared in early 1937.

The wren remained on the farthing for a further twenty-three years, including eight years of the new Queen Elizabeth II's reign, until the coin was finally removed from circulation on 31 December 1960.

The Mint had actually stopped manufacturing farthings four years earlier, when just under two million coins were made, so the latest date

that appears on them is 1956. Overall, during its twenty-year lifetime, roughly 315 million farthings were produced, so that they are certainly not a collector's item. Indeed, if you want to own a 'wren farthing', they can be bought online for between £2 and £20 – something of a bargain, given their rich cultural heritage. Ironically, though, an Edward VIII 'wren farthing' will set you back a cool £13,000.

Yet that's not quite the end of the story. In 1992, more than three decades after the wren became the last (and until now only) British bird to appear on a widely circulated coin of the realm, there was a move to modernise the designs of the one-pound coin, which had first been introduced nine years earlier.

Once again, the Royal Mint Advisory Committee – now under the supervision of Prince Philip, Duke of Edinburgh – was asked to consider a number of images from different designers. Their brief was simple: to create four complementary designs, each representing one of the four nations of the United Kingdom.

One designer, Mary Milner Dickens (who had already created an acclaimed version of the 50p coin), submitted drawings of the coins featuring four species of bird, each chosen because they had made a comeback from the brink of extinction during the twentieth century. They were the avocet (England), osprey (Scotland), red kite (Wales), and roseate tern (Northern Ireland).

The response from the committee was overwhelmingly positive, with the novelist and historian Marina Warner declaring that Dickens had managed to create 'an elegant series of sketches that were in positive danger of producing pleasure'.

It seemed that, for the first time in more than thirty years, a British bird would once again appear on our coins. But at the eleventh hour, the

Chancellor of the Exchequer Norman Lamont unexpectedly chose to intervene, overriding the committee's decision. This led to Marina Warner's resignation in protest, while even the traditionally-minded Duke of Edinburgh was surprised, condemning this late intervention from 'the man from the Treasury'.

Ironically, the reason given for Norman Lamont's rejection of the ornithological designs was that he 'just does not like birds' – even though, like his former Cabinet colleagues Michael Heseltine and Ken Clarke, he is said to be a keen birdwatcher.

So, instead of four beautiful images of British birds, renewing the tradition of the wren on the farthing, the British public ended up with four unimaginative and uninspired heraldic images. These remained in circulation until the old one-pound coin was taken out of circulation (in favour of the new twelve-sided design) in October 2017.

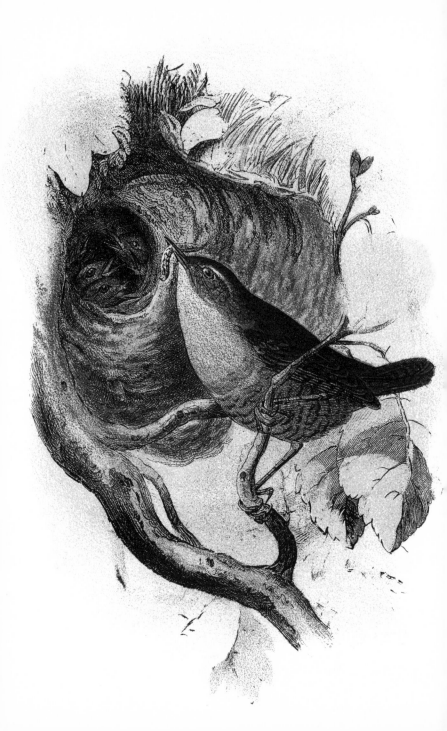

MAY

But now behold the greatest of this train
Of miracles, stupendously minute;
The numerous progeny, claimant for food,
Supplied by two small bills, and feeble wings
Of narrow range. Supplied – ay, duly fed –
Fed in the dark, and yet not one forgot!

James Grahame, *The Birds*
of Scotland, 1806

A dawn chorus in an ancient woodland is, without doubt, one of the wonders not just of the natural world, but of the human sphere too. For this tuning-up of the orchestra, followed by the full-throated concert performance that heralds the new day, is both a biological and cultural phenomenon.

Biological, because the whole purpose of this sonic extravaganza is for the male birds to re-establish their claim to their breeding territory, and their bond with their mate, at the start of each day. Cultural, because few other natural phenomena have captured our collective imaginations quite as strongly. It's also both intense and relaxing – 'intensely relaxing', perhaps – or, as the wildlife sound recordist Gary Moore calls it, 'audio yoga'.

The nineteenth-century American poet Henry Wadsworth Longfellow, best known for his epic poem *The Song of Hiawatha*, summed it up perfectly:

> Think every morning when the sun peeps through
> The dim leaf-latticed windows of the grove,
> How jubilant the happy birds renew
> Their old, melodious madrigals of love!

> And when you think of this, remember too
> 'Tis always morning somewhere, and above
> The awakening continents, from shore to shore,
> Somewhere the birds are singing evermore.

Modern nature writers such as Mark Cocker have picked up this theme: that as the sun continues its slow but inexorable path from east to west each day, a ripple of birdsong gradually encircles the globe. It is a powerful concept, and one that relates to the deep interconnectivity of the natural world. And if these voices should fall silent, as described by the US environmentalist Rachel Carson in her 1962 book *Silent Spring*, then that marks the death-knell not just for birds, but for all living things – including us:

> It was a spring without voices. On the mornings that had once throbbed with the dawn chorus of robins, catbirds, doves, jays, wrens, and scores of other bird voices there was now no sound; only silence lay over the fields and woods and marsh. . .

Fortunately, so far at least, Carson's grim prediction has not come to pass, and on this May Day, in many pagan cultures traditionally the start of summer, the dawn chorus in a wood near my Somerset home is in full voice. And amongst the songsters – competing, as always, to be the loudest and most intense – I can hear several wrens.

You might wonder why, given that these cock wrens are already well into the breeding season, and many have youngsters about to fledge and leave the nest, they would bother to sing at all.

In one sense, they are able to continue to sing because they have the luxury to do so. Now that the sun rises here in the West Country well before 6 a.m., and does not set until almost fifteen hours later, at around 8.30 p.m., all these songsters will have plenty of time to forage for food and go about their other duties during the long daylight hours.

But in truth, they are also still singing because they must. Evolution has driven the production of song as a means to optimise breeding success: even now, another, unmated wren could come in and mate with one of the singer's females, fertilising her eggs so that her second brood belongs to the interloper, and not the incumbent. As the birdsong expert Donald E. Kroodsma pointed out in Cornell University's authoritative *Handbook of Bird Biology*: 'Females . . . sometimes choose to mate with males other than their social partners; much of the male noise we hear during the dawn chorus may actually be geared towards these extra-pair encounters.'

In an apt and striking comparison, Kroodsma went on to compare the male birds' use of sound to an investor, who is managing a portfolio of stocks and shares to maximise financial gain, while competing with other investors who are all trying to achieve the same thing. Hence the cacophony of birdsong that hits us like a wall of sound if we take the trouble to get up early on this, the first day of May.

Meanwhile, back at the nest, five well-grown chicks are almost ready to take the giant leap into the unknown – all the more so as, until now, they have lived inside a domed, enclosed structure with only a small entrance hole, out of which they have semi-emerged to catch their first glimpses of the world outside.

The concept of 'fledging' is a somewhat slippery one. According to the *Oxford English Dictionary* it means 'fit to fly; having the feathers fully developed', but it is often used simply as shorthand for leaving the nest, especially amongst songbirds like the wren.

Fledging does not necessarily imply total independence on the part of young birds. After all, baby ducks, geese, swans and gamebirds (known as 'precocial species') are more or less independent soon after birth, yet do not fledge for several weeks afterwards. Altricial species like the wren are quite different. Indeed, as with many small songbirds, even after fledging and leaving the nest, young wrens are still dependent on their parents for food for one or two weeks afterwards – on occasion even longer.

But before they can be fed outside the nest, the chicks first have to pluck up the courage to depart. This usually happens between fifteen and eighteen days after they hatched, depending how well they have been fed and how large they have managed to grow.

During this relatively short period, they have progressed from Armstrong's blind, naked, 'squirming maggots' to reach the size – and appearance – of their parents. By now, the nest is becoming rather too crowded for their own comfort, especially if all of the original brood of five or six have survived this far. It is hard to imagine how they can continue to stay there, so large have they grown.

The fledging process usually takes place in the morning – but not always very early. It often begins with the female encouraging her brood by flitting around outside the nest, hopping from perch to perch with her tail fully erect, and calling persistently, as she tries to lure them out. She may even bring them morsels of food, to help build up their strength for the big event.

At this point, the male may also show up, as if belatedly making up for his almost total lack of interest in their lives so far. Male

WREN AND YOUNG.

wrens have been observed getting very excited at the prospect of their offspring's appearance outside the nest. They may cling upside down on a twig, leap onto the confused youngsters as they emerge, or even approach the female as if eager to mate. Yet, after all the excitement is over, they often revert to ignoring the chicks once again.

With many other songbirds, such as blue tits or robins, the braver chicks may leave the nest several hours before the final one does so. But wrens, true to their impulsive nature, are different: often all the brood bursts forth from the nest at once, in an explosion of feathers. They accompany this spectacular exit – or entrance, depending on which way you look at it – with an equally impressive burst of sound, a kind of chittering alarm call. The theory behind this is that, by leaving all at once, or very soon after one another, and making a loud noise, the wrens confuse any watching predator.

Once the youngsters have successfully left the nest, their new life begins almost immediately, with the female bringing them food on a regular basis. Unlike many other newly fledged birds, which often move some distance away from the nest, young wrens tend to stay close by, and often stick together, perching in a row on the same branch like miniature tawny owls.

Edward Armstrong waxed both lyrically and anthropomorphically about one such gathering:

> Suddenly the six youngsters came into view in a queer, uneven little procession, squeaking as they hopped up the sloping branch to some twigs a couple of feet away. Filing jerkily upwards, the little group of brown figures reminded me of the Seven Dwarfs in Walt Disney's film.

The Victorian ornithologist William MacGillivray also frequently witnessed the antics of a newly fledged family of wrens 'just come abroad', having been alerted to their presence by the sound they make:

> Walking amongst furze, or broom, or juniper, you are attracted to some bush by hearing issue from it a lively and frequent repetition of a sound which most resembles the syllable *chit*. On going up you perceive an old wren flitting about the twigs, and presently a young one flies off, uttering a stifled *chirr*, to conceal itself among the

bushes. Several follow in succession, while the parents continue to flutter about, in great alarm, uttering their loud *chit, chit, chit*, with indications of varied degrees of excitement.

From now on, having left the safety of the nest, it really is every chick for itself. In an ideal world, the parent wren would know which chick it had just fed, and offer the next morsel of food to a different one, and so on until all the chicks were equally satisfied. But in a world ruled by competition between individuals, rather than some amorphous concept of 'the good of the species', such fairness is off the agenda. Basically, the chick that shouts the loudest gets most food, and will be preferred by the female – even if she offered it food the last time she came, and the time before that.

The chicks signal their hunger, and eagerness to be fed, in the time-honoured way of all young songbirds: they open their mouths as wide as they can, revealing the still-yellow gape that acts as a stimulus to the parent to drop food there. In case that is not enough, the chicks

WREN

also utter a loud and persistent call: a repeated, high-pitched squeak. The call also serves to keep the chicks close to one another, enabling the parent wren to relocate any strays if they happen to wander off, or are dispersed by the approach of a predator like a cat or sparrowhawk.

Wrens are particularly attentive parents at this stage of their offspring's lives. Only dippers, crows and occasionally shrikes continue to feed their fledged chicks for longer than wrens do; the longest known period is of a male wren still feeding a youngster a full month after it had left the nest, but this was exceptional.

During the period when they are being fed by their parents, young wrens do make some effort to find food for themselves. At first, they simply peck randomly at leaves or other objects that attract their attention, but as they grow they begin to learn what is good to eat and what is not.

They also exercise their wings by flying – 'with a blind intentness and an appearance of effort reminiscent of a small boy trying to reach the other side of the swimming bath', as Armstrong so nicely puts it. But a couple of weeks after they have left the nest they are pretty agile, and even able to attempt to hover momentarily on those tiny, whirring wings.

As young wrens get older, they begin to venture farther afield. Often led by their father, and sometimes also by their mother, the youngsters tag along like kids on a woodland walk. Some lag behind, others rush ahead, and explore side alleys – all helping them begin to learn about the world around them. The male will usually keep within his territory on these daily expeditions, while the female may venture into other areas, though is usually careful not to enter the territory of a rival male.

TROGLODYTES EUROPÆUS.

JUNE

. . .for the poor Wren,

The most diminutive of birds, will fight,

Her young ones in her nest, against the owl.

William Shakespeare, *Macbeth*,

Act IV, Scene 2

As with all small birds, the chances of a baby wren surviving to its first birthday are very low. Many birds do not even get as far as fledging, especially if cold or wet weather – or, ironically, a prolonged drought – reduces the availability of food when they are in the nest. Others are seized by a predator soon after leaving or, even if they do make it past the fledging stage, die of starvation during harsh winter weather. Whatever the reasons, according to the BTO a juvenile wren has only a one-in-four chance of surviving to the age of a year old.

Adults do not fare much better than their offspring: in a typical year, fewer than one in three adult wrens survive. Typically, if they get through the dangers in the early part of their life, wrens will reach a lifespan of two years. But the oldest known bird – which was ringed as a chick in the nest in 1997 and then recovered in 2004 – was seven years, three months and six days old.

So what kills them? The number-one factor, as for most small birds, is a shortage of food – especially at crucial times of the year such as midwinter. A wren's energy consumption is phenomenal: it must eat between one-third and half its body weight every single day – the equivalent of an adult human consuming between 100 and 200 Big Macs daily.

The next most likely cause of death, again as with other small birds, is being killed by a predator. This is especially true of wrens, which make their home in our gardens. That's because by providing such a concentrated tapestry of habitats, with food, water, shelter, and places to roost and nest all within a small space, we also create a permanent rolling buffet for predators.

The one advantage the wren has over other garden birds like robins, blackbirds and thrushes is its small size and agility. Its short wings and stubby shape make it very manoeuvrable, and because it spends so much of its time hidden away in the undergrowth, it does not present such an easy target to any potential attacker.

Adult wrens have two very different strategies to avoid predators. Usually, and especially if they have youngsters nearby, they will sound a loud alarm, warning their offspring of danger. But on occasions they will 'freeze' into an immobile pose, remaining completely still for the whole time any predator is in the neighbourhood. For a bird that rarely stays still even for a few seconds, to remain unmoving for so long is very unusual indeed. One adult wren was recorded as maintaining this static pose for almost three minutes – a stupendous feat of self-control for such a little ball of energy.

Predators also take wren eggs, chicks and occasionally adults straight from the nest. Stoats and weasels are good climbers, and weasels are certainly small enough to get inside the entrance hole, as are rats. Snakes, too, occasionally take eggs from birds' nests, especially when they are built close to the ground. And those perennial nest robbers – magpies and jays – have been observed tearing off the dome of a wren's nest with their powerful bills, after which they rapidly make a meal of the unfortunate chicks within.

Parasites, both large and small, can also be a problem. Mites – tiny arthropods distantly related to spiders – can infest a wren's nest so badly that the chicks sicken and die, while wrens are also hosts to three species of feather-lice and two kinds of flea. At the other end of the scale is nest-parasitism by the cuckoo, a problem shared by many other small songbirds.

Given that even a day-old cuckoo chick may weigh 15 grams – about one-and-a-half times the weight of an adult wren – it is perhaps not surprising that the wren is the smallest regular host of the cuckoo in Britain. But compared with the three main victims of the cuckoo – dunnock, reed warbler and meadow pipit, which between them account for the vast majority of records – the wren is rarely chosen.

As they do with their other host species, female cuckoos will carefully watch a pair of wrens, observing where they have made their nest, before dashing in when the parents are away to lay their single egg. Once the baby cuckoo hatches out, it instinctively ejects any of the wrens' own eggs or chicks from the nest, so that it gets all the food brought back by the parents.

Despite the massive size difference – a fully grown cuckoo chick can weigh 100 grams, which is between ten and twelve times the weight of an adult wren – the foster parents do somehow manage to bring back enough food to sustain this monster in their nest. And we know that wrens can raise a baby cuckoo successfully: one ringed in a wren's nest was later recovered at Cap Gris Nez, on the other side of the English Channel, in France.

It is often asked how the single cuckoo chick, which looks so different from the usual brood, can fool its host parents so effectively. One reason is that all parent songbirds are genetically programmed to respond to the sight of any chick's open gape, and fetch food in re-

The Cuckoo.

sponse. Being so large, the cuckoo's gape acts as a 'super-stimulus' to the host parents to bring back even more food.

But, according to the doyen of cuckoo scientists, Nick Davies, this visual stimulus is not always enough on its own to sustain feeding. He and his colleagues discovered that the main stimulus to provoke the hosts to bring back a constant supply of food is, in fact, sound.

In experiments in the field, they found that the cuckoo chick produces a loud and persistent series of begging calls – '*si-si-si-si-si*' – which mimics an entire brood of the host's chicks. 'We suggest that the cuckoo needs vocal trickery,' they concluded, 'to stimulate adequate care to compensate for the fact that it presents a visual stimulus of just one gape.' So sound may be just as important, perhaps even more so, than the visual stimulus.

Edward Armstrong reported several unusual examples of wrens interacting with cuckoos. In one case, a cuckoo laid its egg in a dunnock's nest, which had itself been built on top of a wren's nest containing its young. In an even more unusual instance, a newly fledged brood of young wrens sheltered for the night in a dunnock's nest in which there was also a young cuckoo. When the observer visited one evening to inspect the dunnock's nest, he was astonished to find four baby wrens sheltering under the wing of the cuckoo chick, which he only noticed when their heads popped out, presumably to investigate this human intruder in their midst. Because the young cuckoo's instinct to evict any chicks from its nest disappears after about six days, Armstrong pointed out, it was happy to tolerate these temporary housemates.

In his autobiography *An Eye for a Bird*, the bird photographer Eric Hosking recalled an incident which serves as a warning to this infamous brood parasite. In the autumn of 1931, Hosking and the gamekeeper George Boast inspected more than 150 nest boxes they had erected around Staverton Park, near Daventry in Northamptonshire. In one box they discovered the grisly remains of a bird's skeleton, which Boast immediately realised was that of a young cuckoo inside the nest of a wren. Hosking takes up the tale:

> Presumably the hen cuckoo had projected her egg into the nesting box, the wren had hatched it, and the young cuckoo had been unable to throw out the wren's eggs as these were found broken into tiny pieces. When the cuckoo was fully grown it was, of course, too large to get out of the entrance hole.

As in the case of the wrens roosting under a young cuckoo, occasionally the roles are reversed, with newly fledged wrens found roosting for the night in the nests of other small birds. One family occupied a willow warbler's nest, in which there were four chicks. The parent wren visited the nest with food, but would only give it to her own offspring; whereas the willow warblers seemed happy to feed both their own chicks and the young wrens. Eventually the wrens moved on and, three days later, the willow warbler chicks successfully fledged, apparently none the worse for their shared experience.

Adult wrens have occasionally been seen feeding a range of other baby birds in the vicinity of their nest, including spotted flycatchers, great tits and linnets. Other species of wren in the Americas have also been observed as foster parents. All these cases demonstrate the innate drive found in all songbirds to provide food for any hungry youngster.

Once the youngsters from the first brood are safely fledged, and more or less independent of their parents for food, the adult wrens immediately begin work on their second brood. Often, though, they are in such a hurry to get started that the male will still be feeding his first family of offspring while his mate is busily bringing back feathers to line the new nest.

As we have seen, wrens in the south of their range are more likely to raise two broods than those in the north, or on outlying islands or harsh habitats such as the tundra north of the Arctic Circle – yet two broods have been recorded as far north as Finland.

Generally, a second brood involves more or less starting from scratch – old nests are very occasionally re-used, but only after the male has refurbished them, as they can get very tatty after a whole brood of chicks

has lived there for several weeks. However, successive generations of wrens will re-use the same nest site – a particular nook or cranny that they feel is safe from predators – year after year. Whether these are the offspring from a previous nest, or newcomers attracted by the location, is not known.

During one year in the 1930s, the bird photographer George Marples made an intensive study of a single wren's nest, in which the pair successfully raised a second brood of chicks. What astonished him was the sheer persistence of the adult birds throughout. In one period of just 90 minutes early one morning, when the nest was under construction, it was visited no fewer than twenty-seven times – almost once every three minutes. The male also sang 158 times in eighty minutes, a rate of one song every thirty seconds. Later on, food was taken to the growing chicks every three minutes.

Towards the end of his observations, disaster almost struck when unseasonal summer gales blew the whole nest out of the bush and onto the ground. Fortunately, the chicks had by then grown large enough to leave their wrecked home, and so they survived.

Whether raising their first or second broods, wrens do not always build their own nests. When the opportunity occurs, they will sometimes take over the homes of other birds. The range of species in whose nests wrens have been known to squat is very varied. They include the swallow, house martin, house sparrow and dipper, which you might expect given that these enclosed nests all resemble that of the wren, but also the grey heron – whose nest is a vast superstructure of twigs.

Wrens also often nest close to an eagle's eyrie, perhaps because the much larger eagles lend them a degree of protection against any passing predators. The golden eagle expert Jeff Watson was one who noted that wrens sometimes nest as close as a few metres from the eyrie, and although he had never heard of one actually making its nest inside the huge construction, he speculated that this probably did occur. The scientist Derek Ratcliffe was another to note the proximity of many wrens' nests to eagle eyries, drawing attention to the longstanding mythological association between these two species, which I shall explore in the next chapter.

The only definitive account of a wren actually building its nest inside a golden eagle's eyrie comes from Dorothy Hosking, the wife of bird photographer Eric. True to form, Hosking had taken his wife to Scotland on their honeymoon – not, as she might have hoped, for a relaxing visit to a luxury hotel, but to photograph golden eagles. Dorothy, who fortunately seems to have shared her husband's enthusiasms, takes up the story, in this extract from her diary, wryly entitled *I Married a Naturalist*:

> To our delight we discovered a wren had built her small nest in the large structure of the eagle's eyrie. This wee bird seemed much more concerned with her family's welfare than the golden eagle was with hers. Back and forth she flew, and sometimes the cock would sing his sweet shrill song. I always marvel how so small a bird can sing so loudly.

Female wren brings lining material to her nest

By the end of June, though sometimes as late as August, many wrens – especially those in the south of Britain – will already have successfully raised two broods of young. From then on, both young and adult wrens become – like most other songbirds – more and more elusive. That's because they are now undergoing the process of moult, re-growing their plumage to face the rigours of the autumn and winter to come.

Midsummer is the ideal time to moult: there is plenty of available food, and long daylight hours in which to forage for it. Also, the foliage of bushes, shrubs and trees is now at its thickest, which means that, as they lose their old feathers and grow new ones, wrens are able to hide away even more effectively than usual. The juvenile birds, which only left the nest a few weeks before, undergo what is known as a 'post-juvenile moult' into the adult plumage, after which they look exactly like their parents.

Wrens also fall silent at this time of year: although on my local patch or in my garden I occasionally hear a wren singing in early July, they usually don't start again until September. They then continue singing regularly for the rest of the year, though far less frequently and less intensely than during the breeding season.

From now on, they have very different priorities. Summer may still have a long way to run, but it is not so long before autumn arrives, and with it another great challenge in the life of this small bird: to survive until the next breeding season.

The Marriage.

JULY

The world is grown so bad,

That wrens make prey where eagles dare not perch.

William Shakespeare, *Richard III*,

Act I, Scene 3

Birds have always inspired myths and legends, in virtually every one of the world's cultures, including our own. Some stories are specific to one culture, place or time, but others are found – with a few local variations – in many different parts of the world, at various stages of human history. One of these is the tale of the King of Birds.

The story goes like this. One day, having seen that mankind had its own ruler, all the birds gathered together to choose a king. But they could not agree over how to actually select their monarch. Some argued that the most beautiful bird should win; others wanted the one with the sweetest song. Some called for the strongest bird to rule over them; others disagreed, instead proposing that King of the Birds should be the one that could fly the farthest.

Finally, after much debate, they decided to ask the wise old owl to choose for them. He considered for a while, and then announced that the winner should be the species that was able to fly higher than all the others, as that would bring it closest to God.

The other birds agreed, and so each flapped its wings and started to fly up into the heavens. Gradually, one by one, their strength failed them, and they drifted back down to the ground. But one bird – the mighty eagle – was still flying higher and higher, by now almost out of sight.

Looking up, the rest of the birds hailed the eagle as their king, an honour the now exhausted bird gratefully acknowledged, before preparing to return to earth. But unbeknownst to either him, or the rest of the birds, the tiny wren had tucked himself away beneath the eagle's feathers. Just as the eagle reached his highest point, the wren popped out from his hiding place, and flew even higher.

When the wren and the eagle had come back down onto the ground, the wren spoke first, claiming his rightful place as the King of Birds. The eagle, still angry and being so deceived, stayed silent. But the other birds still could not decide, so once again they consulted the owl. He gave his final verdict: that although the wren had indeed gone higher than the eagle, it had not done so under its own steam, and so the eagle was the rightful King of Birds.

In disgrace, the wren sneaked off into the undergrowth, and never tried to fly so high again – which explains why wrens always creep about, as if embarrassed by their pretensions in trying to be king.

In another version of the same tale, from a medieval German source, the eagle is so angry that it swipes the wren with its powerful wing, damaging the smaller bird's wings and tail, so that from that day forth it is unable to fly further than a short distance. Yet another iteration has the eagle place a curse on the wren, so that again, it is unable to fly very far: this explains why the wren 'can never fly over a hedge, but always goes through it'.

The story also appears in the tales of the nineteenth-century German Brothers Grimm, but with a twist. After the wren has proclaimed itself the King of Birds, the others set a new test, designed to foil its plans: whoever can go deepest underground will now be the ruler. But the crafty wren immediately plunges down a tiny mouse hole, and once again proclaims himself to be king.

This time the other birds are even angrier, so they imprison him inside the hole, and place the owl outside as a guard. But when the owl falls asleep, the wren manages to escape. As a punishment for the owl's carelessness, he is condemned to live a permanently nocturnal existence, while the wren must, from that day onward, hide himself away to avoid being recaptured.

In a Welsh variation on the theme of the wren needing to be punished for its hubris and arrogance, the other birds try to drown the poor bird in a pan filled with their own tears. Yet again, the owl inadvertently foils this plan by clumsily overturning the pan, allowing the wren to escape; and as before, the owl earns its fellow birds' displeasure and must only emerge under cover of darkness.

What all these different versions of the same story have in common is that they seek to provide a logical explanation for the wren's unusual and very specific habits: its tendency to stay close to the ground, to fly low, only over a short distance, and to creep around or hide away in the undergrowth. All of these are, of course, evolutionary adaptations to the wren's way of life; knowing this, however, does not diminish the wonder we feel at the imaginative invention of our ancestors.

The story of the King of Birds is a very ancient one, found in many European and North American cultures. It is mentioned in the works of the Greek philosopher Aristotle and the Roman writer Pliny. Some believe it was originally one of Aesop's fables, dating back to Ancient Greece in the sixth and seventh centuries BC. The Roman essayist Plutarch, writing in the first century AD (roughly 700 years after Aesop), certainly thought so, when he wrote of 'Aesop's wren who was

carried up on the eagle's shoulders, then suddenly flew out and got ahead of him'.

Intriguingly, though, the story may actually be even older than that. In her masterful study of the wren in world folklore, *Hunting the Wren*, the US anthropologist Elizabeth Atwood Lawrence noted that many of Aesop's fables could have originated in much earlier stories from the cradle of human civilisation, Mesopotamia (part of present-day Iraq). That would mean that some of these tales – including the story of the eagle and the wren – might date back as far as the second millennium BC, at least 3,000 years ago.

This or similar stories also appeared in other parts of the world, though often with very different participants. Thus, in China, the contestants were the ox and the rat, with the fastest animal winning the race (presumably showing that the rat's cunning will always triumph over the ox's strength). In a Mayan legend from Central America, the contest was between the roadrunner and the quetzal, and involved the quetzal stealing the roadrunner's feathers in order to win the avian equivalent of a beauty contest.

All these stories show that, from the very earliest times, our ancestors tried to explain the workings of the natural world around them. Birds, being common, easy to see and more or less ubiquitous, were placed at the centre of many of these myths and stories. In Britain and Europe especially, where the wren is one of the commonest and most widespread birds of all, it is hardly surprising that it features so prominently in our folklore, culture and literature.

There is, however, one tiny question mark when it comes to the story of the eagle and the wren. As most birders are aware, the goldcrest belongs to the genus *Regulus*, which translates from the Latin as 'little king' – hence an alternative name for the goldcrest and its relatives, 'kinglet'.

Today, this term is confined to North America, where it refers to two close relatives of the goldcrest, the ruby-crowned and golden-crowned kinglets. But in Victorian times it was widely used as a name for the goldcrest, as in the observation from the ornithologist William Yarrell that 'The little Golden Crested Regulus, or Kinglet, has a soft and pleasing song.'

Since the eagle is Europe's largest bird, and the goldcrest the smallest, might it not be possible that the 'wren' in all these stories was originally meant to be a goldcrest? After all, until the late nineteenth century, and occasionally beyond, the goldcrest was still known as the 'golden-crested wren'; in addition, goldcrests are just as skulking in their habits as the wren, indeed perhaps even more so.

The waters are further muddied when we discover that the goldcrest is often referred to as the 'king of birds' in various European folk tales, while in several Scandinavian languages the name for the goldcrest translates as 'king's bird' or 'little king'. In Swedish, therefore, it is *kungsfågel*, while in Danish and Norwegian it is the *fuglekinge*. However, other European languages, including German, Swedish, French, Spanish and Italian, have folk names for the wren based on the notion that it is the king of birds, though as even Edward Armstrong admitted, 'one could hardly discover any bird whose appearance and behaviour less suggest a claim to royal honours.'

In some ways, it doesn't really matter if the bird in the myth is the wren or the goldcrest; what is more relevant is that despite their small size and furtive habits – or perhaps even because of them – both birds have a central importance in British and European culture and folklore.

References to the wren can be found in many different cultures within our islands, including Welsh and Scottish and Irish Gaelic folk tales. In Wales, the wren is seen as a bird able to foretell the future, like the druid priests, hence the Welsh name *drui-eun*, which translates as 'Druid bird'.

In Scotland, however, wrens are often treated with rather less reverence: one saying, from the Hebridean island of South Uist, translates from the Scottish Gaelic as 'A big egg will never come from the wren's backside' – presumably meaning that nothing grand will ever come from something so small: the diametric opposite of the saying 'From little acorns big oaks will grow.' This may be because, according to some folklorists, the wren is thought to bring bad luck in Scotland (except if it builds its nest around your home or inside a hayrick), whereas the robin brings good fortune.

Another Scottish Gaelic proverb provides a variation on the same theme, translating as 'There never came a hearty fart from a wren's arse,' meaning that a small present rarely contains anything very special. And there are several folk-tales founded upon the wren's agility to punch above its weight: sometimes literally, as when this tiny bird manages to kill a horse and a bull, yet also metaphorically, when it outwits that most cunning of animals, the fox.

In Ireland in particular, where the wren is one of the most common and abundant of all small birds, it is the subject of countless myths and legends. Wrens were widely regarded as having the power of prophecy – possibly because they sing so loudly. In a further variation on the tale, it was believed that, depending on which direction the bird's song was coming from, the nature of that prophecy would change from good to bad.

The wren also features in the ancient 'ogham alphabet', a form of written Irish dating back almost 2,000 years to the first century AD. According to the Irish naturalist and folklore-collector Niall Mac Coitir, the wren, which stood for the letter 'D', 'is said to depict rebellion, independence of spirit and freedom' – all qualities which reflect this little bird's feisty character.

Wrens were often regarded as special, and also – along with other small birds such as the robin – in need of protection. This view is at the heart of William Blake's poem 'Auguries of Innocence', published in 1863, six decades after it was written, and some thirty-six years after the poet's death. Amongst several other couplets that have ended up as well-known quotations (including 'A robin redbreast in a cage, puts all heaven in a rage') are the lines:

He who shall hurt the little wren
Shall never be belov'd by men.

Many traditional country verses reinforce this message: that if you
should harm a wren – or worse still, kill it – you will come to a bad end,
as in this fine piece of rural doggerel:

I never take away their nest nor try
To catch the old ones, lest a friend should die.
Dick took a wren's nest from his cottage side,
And ere a twelvemonth past his mother died!

Ancient silver wren brooch

Those who dared to disobey this rule could find themselves shunned by the community: in Cornwall, parents might tell their children not to play with anyone who had done such a terrible deed. It was widely believed that if a boy killed a wren he would die before he reached adulthood, while it was also said that if someone took a wren's eggs their fingers would turn crooked. Powerful stuff.

On the other hand, if a wren made its nest in or around your home, this was supposed to bring good luck. The folk name 'Our Lady's Hen' was widespread, and across the Channel in Normandy the wren was referred to as '*la poulette au bon Dieu*', which translates as 'God's little hen'.

In Devon – and especially around the coast – it was widely believed that if you carried a wren's feather when you went to sea, this would protect you against drowning. Another version of this story, noted in the Revd Charles Swainson's 1886 work *The Folk Lore and Provincial Names of British Birds*, reported that Devon herring fishermen would, just before they set off, pluck the feathers from a live wren and toss them into the air. Depending on whether they fell to the deck or blew away in the wind, the fishing would be successful or fruitless. Wrens' tail-feathers were also used for a more practical purpose, to make fishing-flies to catch trout.

The seventeenth-century ornithologists John Ray and Francis Willughby pointed out that some ancient civilisations also considered wrens to have medicinal value, as in this 'recipe':

It perfectly cures the stone of the kidneys of bladder being salted or eaten raw, or being burnt in a pot close covered, and the ashes of one whole bird taken at once . . . or lastly being roasted whole, only the feathers being plucked off and cast away.

We have long since ceased to use wrens – and other birds – as medicinal cures, but as Elizabeth Atwood Lawrence noted:

> Such convictions about the wren's capacities to punish or reward human beings demonstrate not only the power attributed to the tiny bird, but reflect general faith in the reciprocal relationship between humankind and nature that was once taken for granted.

We sometimes scoff at these superstitions today, but for our ancestors they represented a system of beliefs and worldview that inextricably connected them with the natural world, in a way that many of us still strive to recapture.

Perhaps the best-known rhyme about the wren links it to Britain's favourite bird, the robin:

> The Robin Redbreast and the Wren
> Are God Almighty's cock and hen.

In some versions this concludes with the dire warning:

> Him that harries at their nest,
> Never shall his soul have rest.

Other sayings with a similar admonition include 'Kill a robin or a wren, never prosper, boy or man,' and the even starker 'Cursed is the man, who kills a robin or a wren.'

The usual interpretation of such sententiousness is that all God's creatures – especially tiny, weak, defenceless birds – deserve divine protection. That was certainly the view of George Scott-Moncrieff, a Scottish writer and editor who in 1951 produced a slender volume retelling the story which poet Robert Burns reputedly used to tell his children, entitled *The Marriage of Robin Redbreast and The Wren*. This in turn was based on a traditional verse, 'The Courtship and Marriage of Cock Robin and Jenny Wren', which sadly ends (like the rhyme 'Who Killed Cock Robin?') in the violent death of the groom, who is shot by an arrow.

In another traditional verse, the robin protects the wren when she is ill:

> Little Jenny Wren fell sick upon a time,
> When in came Robin Redbreast and brought her sops and wine,
> 'Eat, Jenny, drink, Jenny, all shall be thine!'
> 'Thank you, Robin, kindly, you shall be mine.'

But as the wren recovers, she turns the tables on her protector:

> Then Jenny Wren got better, and stood upon her feet,
> And said to Robin Redbreast, 'I love thee not a bit.'
> Then Robin he was angry, and flew upon a pole,
> 'Hoot upon thee! Fie upon thee! Ungrateful soul.'

The various rhymes and stories coupling these two species appear to suggest that our ancestors mistakenly thought the wren to be the mate of the robin, which sounds rather unlikely. Surely, as W. B. Lockwood surmised, the coupling arose from the fortunate coincidence that while the redbreast (as the robin was then known) had been given the

masculine nickname Robin, the wren had earned the female nickname Jenny. 'Wren' happening to rhyme with 'hen' made it even easier to pair the two together. In other words, explains Elizabeth Atwood Lawrence, 'The superstition did not give rise to the verse, but rather the verse created the superstition.'

Nowadays, with such beliefs having been mostly long forgotten, we rarely consider these two birds to have a special relationship. But for a brief period towards the end of the nineteenth century, the robin and the wren frequently appeared together on Christmas cards.

This was based on an ancient belief that the wren represented the Old Year, and the robin the New, but the cards themselves give little away about the dark nature of this particular conjunction of the two species. For this time the wren and the robin are not lovers or spouses, but father and son, and the robin, which symbolises the hope brought by the New Year, must kill his father the wren so that his reign as King of the Old Year can end, and the world can start afresh.

On one particular card, a robin and two wrens are depicted covering a doll half-buried in the snow. This is a clear reference to the folk-tale 'Babes in the Wood', itself based on the belief that robins (and presumably wrens) cover up dead bodies with leaves to protect them from view.

These darker sides of wren folklore find their apogee in the extraordinary story of the Wren Hunt, which I shall save for the final chapter.

AUGUST

Like spume and spindrift, the pearls of wrens' eggs
were found in the lower depths or ledges
of a cliff, not far from where shags and guillemots' legs
stand till that hour they come to crack and shells
reveal these small birds that bear frail
notes, celebrating on each cleit and wall
their triumph at being born,
having survived these nights when stone and crags are torn
like shells below the cudgels of a storm.

Donald Murray, 'Wrens',
The Guga Stone, 2013

The impossibly tall stacks loom out of the mist, in another of Donald Murray's numinous phrases, 'like Atlantis'. This lost world is shrouded in both mist and mystery: the tiny sea-washed islet of Rockall aside, the archipelago of St Kilda is the remotest, and most inaccessible, place in the British Isles.

St Kilda first came to the world's notice in the latter years of the seventeenth century, when the early explorer Martin Martin first made landfall there, and wrote about his epic journey in *A Late Voyage to St Kilda*, published in 1698.

Martin had endured a horrendous crossing: at one stage during their storm-tossed journey things got so bad that he and his shipmates 'laid aside all hopes of life'. But his account didn't put people off from wanting to visit, and since then, St Kilda has been a magnet for those souls – and there are many of us – who suffer from what Lawrence Durrell called 'islomania': an insatiable attraction to islands.

In 2002, just over 300 years after Martin made his epic voyage here, I achieved one of my lifetime's ambitions by getting to St Kilda myself, to film an episode of the TV series *Bill Oddie Goes Wild*. We almost never made it: our journey, on the yacht *Silurian*, lasted four days, which was one day longer than I had taken, earlier that same year, to travel all the way to Antarctica. The trip was also marked by high winds, rolling waves and, for two of my colleagues – sound recordist Chris Watson and Bill Oddie himself – chronic seasickness.

The crossing of the Minch, the sea channel between the mainland and the Outer Hebrides, was pretty terrifying, with high waves tossing and turning the small yacht for hours on end. But by the time we reached the Sound of Harris, on our third evening after leaving home, conditions had finally changed for the better. The sea was like the proverbial millpond, the sun shone clear and strong in the west and, as Arctic terns swooped and dived around our boat, the way was finally clear for us to sail overnight for our ultimate destination.

As dawn broke the next morning, with the sea still flat calm, we anchored the yacht in Village Bay, on the island of Hirta. This was where the inhabitants of St Kilda, christened the 'bird people', lived – and from where, on a fine, sunny day in late August 1930, they finally left their home behind forever.

But evidence of the many centuries they lived here remains, in the form of ruined houses, drystone walls, and the strange stone structures known as 'cleits'. It was inside these that the islanders stored the seabirds they had collected and killed during the summer season of plenty: mostly puffins and gannets. Their corpses were then dried inside the cleits, and would sustain the people during the cheerless autumn and winter months, until the birds returned to breed again the following spring.

When we arrived, none of this was visible, as the island was shrouded in fog, so we had to rely for first impressions on our hearing. Listening carefully, I could make out the gentle wash of the waves along the shoreline, and the distant calls of countless seabirds: puffins, guillemots, razorbills and fulmars squabbling over their tiny territories. For a moment, I imagined I could hear the conversations of those ghostly islanders, who for centuries had managed to cling onto a harsh existence here, on the very edge of the known world.

And then I heard it. The unmistakable song of a cock wren, floating through the mist towards us. The sound was both familiar – loud, and packed with the characteristic trills, arpeggios and onrush of notes squeezed into an impossibly small space – and yet unfamiliar; somehow not quite the same as the wrens I had been listening to in my garden just a few days before: to my ear, a little less varied in tone.

It was this difference in sound, together with subtle but more definite variations in the size and plumage of these island birds, that first led the Victorian scientist and explorer Henry Seebohm to declare that these particular wrens belonged to a unique species, found here and nowhere else on the planet. In 1884, he christened it *Troglodytes hirtensis*: the St Kilda wren. However, just two years later another ornithologist, Henry Dresser, reclassified it as the *hirtensis* subspecies of *Troglodytes troglodytes*.

Whether the St Kilda wren's song is all that different from the birds in the rest of Britain remains a moot point. William Eagle Clarke had his doubts; yet Tom Harrisson and John Buchan, who visited the islands on a joint Oxford and Cambridge expedition in the summer of 1931, believed it was. In a detailed paper about the bird's habits and status they stated that 'it has a finer, yet weaker tone, more musical and continuous, less throaty' than the song of mainland birds. To confuse things still further, other observers have remarked that the St Kilda wren's song was much louder and more powerful.

Some of this could, of course, be explained by the habitat and surroundings: any bird that competes to be heard above the heavy waves and high winds typical of these islands is likely to sing more loudly and enthusiastically than one in my quiet Somerset garden, for example.

Bill Oddie certainly thought so: in his broadcast on the St Kilda wren for BBC Radio 4's *Tweet of the Day*, he pointed out that 'they have to make themselves heard above the crashing of waves and the yelping of seabirds.' Chris Watson says that, to his ear, 'the St Kilda birds have less variety than their mainland cousins; they have the same basic "template", but the phrases are more uniform.' Perhaps the definitive judgement should come, as it so often does, from Edward Armstrong, who declared that 'The song is more musical, less mechanical, and less shrill than that of the European Wren.'

On my own visit to St Kilda, moments after we had first heard the wren's song floating towards us, the mist miraculously began to clear, and the sun illuminated the scene before us. It reminded me, oddly, of a visit I had made many years earlier to the Mayan temple at Palenque, in the heart of Mexico's Yucatán Peninsula. I felt that same peculiar sense of being in the midst of a lost civilisation, weighing down the landscape with its unseen, yet incredibly potent, presence.

The wren sang again; and for the first time I glimpsed it briefly as it hopped up onto the wall of the island cemetery, packed with graves and headstones commemorating the many generations of people who lived and died here.

I moved closer, until I was almost at the wall itself, when out of the corner of my eye I noticed a distinct movement. The wren had momentarily stopped singing and was foraging for tiny insects amongst the greenish-grey, lichen-covered stones. If the song had struck me as subtly different from that of this bird's mainland cousins, then that was nothing compared to its appearance.

Judging the size of a bird – especially a lone individual seen in a very unusual habitat – is always tricky. Yet the moment I saw the St Kilda wren, I realised it was obviously larger and bulkier than the wrens back home. In the absence of other small birds, it seemed to rule its little kingdom: hopping confidently, even proprietorially, from wall to wall, and tombstone to tombstone.

Like size, the colour and shade of a bird can also be difficult to assess: the light at different times of day, and in new and unfamiliar locations, can alter our perception hugely. But again, I was sure that this bird was paler, greyer and far colder in shade than those little rufous bundles of feathers I have seen elsewhere in Britain.

Ad. m. (upper) Juv. (lower) Ad. f.   Ad. m.   Ad. f.
WREN (⅓)   SHETLAND WREN   ST. KILDA WREN

Writing in 1884, Richard Barrington, one of the first people to make close observations of wrens on St Kilda, suggested that the birds may have become paler and larger because of their exposure to a more humid, maritime environment. The St Kilda wren also conforms to Bergmann's Rule, in which the farther north you go, the larger the individuals of a particular species get. That's because their greater ratio of volume to surface area enables them to retain heat for longer, which might then make the difference between life and death in the bleak St Kilda winter.

Other observers have got the same sense of a larger, bulkier, greyer and paler bird. In the authoritative *Handbook of British Birds*, published from 1938 to 1941, Bernard Tucker summed up the differences as being 'rather greyer-brown above and paler below than common form, with barring heavier, and more extensive on mantle', while the *Handbook*'s editor Harry Witherby added that the St Kilda birds are 'never so rufous nor so variable as typical form, and barring considerably heavier'. He went on to note several other small but significant differences, such as a whiter supercilium, and paler, less buff underparts.

The St Kilda wren is notably larger. While the wings of typical mainland wrens are on average 47.5 mm long, those of the St Kilda wrens are 50.2 mm; the bill, too, is longer, ranging from 13.5 to 16 mm in length, compared to 13.3–14.8 mm for mainland wrens.

But by far the greatest difference is in the comparative weights: whereas typical wrens tip the scales at between 9 and 11 grams, the St Kilda wrens weigh in at a whopping 12.5–14.5 grams – that's roughly one-third heavier.

Writing in *British Birds* in 2011, Will Miles – who spent four consecutive summers living on the islands – pointed out how these small differences in size and plumage became far more significant when he finally saw the St Kilda wren for himself:

I was initially surprised by their appearance and plumage, being far more distinctive than I was expecting. In the field the birds looked startlingly large, much bigger – and longer-bodied – than other UK subspecies, as well as very long-billed. The general impression seemed unfamiliar, more creeper-like than wren. Most distinctive in adults was just how pale, cold and stony were the grey tones of the head, underparts and mantle.

Such pronounced differences in song, size, structure and plumage between wrens on St Kilda and elsewhere in the British Isles, might lead one to assume that they have been isolated from one another for millions – perhaps even tens of millions – of years.

Yet until the end of the last Ice Age, roughly 12,000 years ago, the northern parts of Europe were under a thick layer of ice, so it seems likely that, as the ice retreated and songbirds such as the wren recolonised Britain, these birds would not have reached St Kilda and other outlying islands until perhaps 5,000 years ago.

Five thousand years doesn't sound like a very long time to enable the wrens on St Kilda to evolve so much, but recent studies on Darwin's finches on the Galápagos Islands suggest that evolutionary changes – sometimes into what may be entirely new species – can occur much more rapidly than we once assumed. Indeed, if the conditions are significantly different from the norm, which they certainly were on St Kilda, they can happen within just a few generations.

*

The first people to observe wrens on St Kilda were surprised that the birds were there at all, as the islands are 64 km (40 miles) from the nearest land, North Uist in the Outer Hebrides. As Kenneth Macaulay wrote in his 1764 book *The History of St Kilda*, 'How these little birds . . . could have flown thither, or whether they went accidentally in boats, I leave undetermined.'

But fly they did and, having reached this new land, they initially fared rather well. Yet ironically, it was Henry Seebohm's hasty declaration, claiming that the wrens on St Kilda were a new and unique species, that almost did for the bird. Following his publication, the Victorian mania for collecting the skins and eggs of rare birds reared its ugly head, and as a direct consequence, just four years later, in 1888, the St Kilda wren was thought to be almost extinct. In the words of one later commentator, 'in those bad old days . . . a new name for a new bird was sufficient to set the ornithological underworld aflame with lust and greed.'

For the islanders, then living a harsh, hand-to-mouth existence based mainly on collecting seabirds, which were then utilised for food, fuel, clothing and even medicine, the sudden demand for this familiar little bird was nothing short of a godsend. One entrepreneurial St Kildan demanded one guinea (21 shillings) for each adult wren, and 12s 6d for the young – at today's values, roughly equivalent to £120 and £72 respectively – a small fortune for such a poor people.

With the bird's small and geographically restricted population, this state of affairs could not be sustained for long: indeed, at one stage, the conservationist W. H. Hudson went as far as to declare that the St Kilda wren was already extinct. Then, at the eleventh hour, an unlikely saviour appeared: the Right Hon Sir Herbert Eustace Maxwell, 7th Baronet of Monreith.

Sir Herbert was a Conservative politician, novelist and artist who, appalled by the wanton killing of the islands' wrens, put forward a bill in Parliament, which was eventually passed as the Wild Birds (St Kilda) Protection Act, 1904.

Once the Act had become law, the natural proclivities of all wrens meant that the population had recovered within a decade. In 1914, when the Duchess of Bedford visited the islands in her yacht (not on some dilettante pleasure trip, as the Duchess was a well-known ornithologist), she reported seeing the St Kilda wren in good numbers.

When the young David Lack arrived on the islands on the 1931 Oxford and Cambridge expedition, he decided to attempt the first ever complete survey of the population of the St Kilda wren. This task was made even trickier by the birds' choice of habitat: although I watched them in the comparatively sheltered and accessible surroundings of the village cemetery, they mostly nest along the precipitous and dangerous sea-cliffs around the edges of the islands.

In total, Lack and his fellow observers tallied sixty-eight breeding pairs: forty-five on the main island of Hirta, eleven on Dun, nine on Soay and just three on the island of Boreray, home to one of the world's largest gannet colonies. This was, Lack knew, a gross underestimate, but it was a start.

A quarter of a century later, in 1957, Kenneth Williamson carried out a far more detailed survey, coming up with the figure of 233 breeding pairs. That's very close to the latest estimate reported in the authoritative 2007 work *The Birds of Scotland*, of between 230 and 250 pairs, almost half of which are on the main island of Hirta. Two or three pairs also nest annually near the summit of Stac an Armin, at a height of almost 200 metres (650 feet) – about four times the height of Nelson's Column.

But finding all the archipelago's wrens is an impossible task. As Williamson later noted, surveying potential nesting sites is daunting and sometimes dangerous, and 'has involved many enthusiasts in much scrambling and foot-slogging around Hirta's majestic perimeter, peering over dizzy edges for a glimpse of a feathered, mouse-like form, or cocking an ear for a wisp of song hundreds of feet below'. Williamson also presciently suggested that an accurate survey of the islands' wren population 'would be a major undertaking, involving several days' stay ashore, and for that reason may never be carried out'. So far, at least, his prediction has proved quite correct, and we still do not have truly accurate figures.

In the 1931 survey, Lack's colleagues Harrisson and Buchan noted that all the pairs they had found were nesting in just three distinct habitats: twelve in and around the now unoccupied buildings, nineteen on steep cliffs, and no fewer than thirty-seven – more than half the total – in and around the puffin colonies, on the grassy slopes near the summit of the cliffs and crags.

This proximity to puffins, which nest in burrows they dig using their powerful claws, was no accident. St Kilda's 100,000-plus pairs of puffins feed their single chick on fish – mainly sand-eels – and both chicks and adult birds produce copious amounts of droppings. As a result, there are numerous insects in and around the puffin colonies, providing the wrens with a reliable and abundant source of food when feeding their own chicks.

As Williamson noted, 'insects are most plentiful at the puffinries, attracted by the lush vegetation which thrives on the guano-enriched soil, and especially by carrion of various kinds – such as sand-eels dropped from the puffins' bills, the corpses of adult birds slain by the gulls, and of young birds which die outside their burrows.'

Will Miles also observed that St Kilda wrens often nest close to three other hole-nesting seabirds – Manx shearwater, and European and Leach's storm petrels – presumably for the same reason.

Like all wrens, the St Kilda race is mainly insectivorous. But it is hardly surprising that the birds take a rather different range of food from their mainland cousins. Observations suggest that as well as small beetles, flies and spiders, they also feed their young on the caterpillars of a species of noctuid moth, as well as earwigs and centipedes. In the years following the islands' evacuation, some wrens still entered the now dilapidated stone houses to find flies inside.

Nesting materials are also different – again, hardly a surprise, given the singular environment in which the birds live. So the males use coarse grasses and bracken to build the nest, which the female then lines with the feathers of fulmars and puffins, two of the most numerous seabirds on the islands.

In the complete absence of trees, most nests are constructed in crevices on cliff-faces, gaps in the walls of the cleits or, rather picturesquely, tucked beneath the myriad clumps of sea pink (thrift), which add a welcome splash of colour to the clifftops from late spring and throughout the summer.

Like the mainland birds, St Kilda wrens lay between four and six eggs, which are, however, considerably larger and have bolder reddish-brown markings. The clutch is also laid much later, usually in late May, June or early July (though this does vary, depending on the prevailing weather conditions in any particular summer).

Ultimately, the timing of breeding for these island birds is governed by the availability of food, and so is closely tied in with the puffins'

PLATE 33—WREN FEEDING HER YOUNG: A. W. Seaby

breeding cycle. By the time the puffins leave the islands in early August, the wrens have also finished breeding, and are feeding well-grown young outside the nest. However, in January 1959, a St Kilda wren was seen building a nest inside a large jam jar propped up against one of the village walls. Not surprisingly, it did not go on to lay any eggs there.

There is usually only one brood and, as one would expect from the inhospitable habitat and short window of opportunity to raise the chicks, St Kilda wrens are strictly monogamous, unlike their louche southern relatives. Neither do they waste any precious time building cock's nests and, after the eggs have hatched, the males take a full part in feeding duties.

The St Kilda wren is one of no fewer than four different island races of the wren found in the British Isles. The others are the Hebridean wren, of the race *hebridensis*, found throughout the Outer Hebrides (Western Isles); the Shetland wren, *zetlandicus*, found throughout our northernmost archipelago; and the Fair Isle wren, *fridariensis*, confined to that tiny speck of land between Shetland and Orkney. The Fair Isle wren really is on the edge of existence, with a current population of thirty or so pairs – up from a low of just ten singing males in 1981.

The Shetland wren is, according to David Bannerman, strikingly darker than its St Kilda cousin, and quite close to it in size. The Hebridean wren, found throughout the Western Isles, is also darker than both the mainland and St Kilda wrens, and has a much shorter bill than both. The Fair Isle wren – which was not even described as a potentially separate race until 1951 – is actually closer in appearance to the St Kilda wren than to its Shetland cousins less than 40 km (25 miles) across the sea, being noticeably paler and greyer. Yet having seen all these different races, on various visits to our offshore islands, I would be pushed to pick them out in an avian identity parade.

The existence of so many island races in the comparatively well-studied environs of the British Isles makes me wonder, indeed, whether there might be many more as yet unknown ones, somewhere in the less frequently visited parts of the Eurasian wren's vast range?

Scientific scrutiny has failed to demote any of the wren's UK island races, and merge them with our own familiar mainland ones. In fact, the recent trend towards 'splitting' existing species, and promoting distinctive races to full species status, is making the odds against at least the St Kilda wren becoming a new species, *Troglodytes hirtensis* – and vindicating Henry Seebohm in the process – look shorter by the day.

As Jeremy Mynott pointed out in *Birdscapes*, fundraising to support what he calls 'a proper species' is much easier than trying to raise money

St. Kilda wren at its nest

to conserve a mere subspecies: 'St Kilda wrens,' he comments, 'should follow this debate with interest.' He does, however, go on to suggest that the St Kilda wren's future elevation to a full species would be far more likely if the bird happened to be larger and more charismatic. He may well be right.

But whether a full species or 'just' a subspecies, the importance of the St Kilda wren goes beyond its biological categorisation, says Mynott, and into full-blown symbolism.

The bird is surely the wild spirit of the place. . . The wren seems elemental – a tiny persistent life in these desolate landscapes governed by the huge impersonal forces of wind, tide and weather.

After just two full days on St Kilda, during which we were blessed with some of the loveliest weather I have ever enjoyed in the Scottish Highlands and Islands, we had to depart. As we boarded our yacht, moored out in the natural harbour of Village Bay, I could hear, above the constant cries of the gulls, that familiar yet subtly different trill, wafting across the sea from the cliffs above us.

A St Kilda wren was, I fancied, wishing us a safe, calm voyage home.

SEPTEMBER

The *Trochilus* [Wren] inhabits shrubberies and holes and cannot easily be caught. Now it is shy and of a feeble habit, but endowed with great ability of getting food and knowledge of its craft.

Aristotle, *History of Animals*, 4th century BC,
translated by William Turner, 1544

On my local patch, a hidden corner of the vast reedbeds that make up the Avalon Marshes in Somerset, September is usually the quietest month of the year. The cohort of warblers that breed here in the spring and summer – up to ten different species in a good year – has long since fallen silent, and most have now departed south to their winter quarters in Africa or south-west Europe. But the noisy groups of ducks – including wigeon, teal and shoveler – that come here from the north and east, together with vast flocks of redwings and fieldfares from Iceland and Scandinavia, have yet to arrive.

Sometimes I can walk all the way around the woods and reedbeds without hearing a single bird sing, though the resident Cetti's warblers usually contribute the occasional explosive burst from their hiding places in the brambles. If I do hear a more conventional song, it is usually the sweet, rather plaintive sounds of the robin, a bird well known for its habit of defending territories, and regularly singing, throughout the autumn and winter.

Yet there is another bird here, a bird almost as hard to see as the elusive Cetti's, which also gives away its presence with a burst of sound: the wren. Sometimes it does so with a loud, clear song: that series of trills and whistles I haven't heard since late spring. After all, like the robin – a bird with which it is so often linked – wrens hold territories in autumn and winter.

But more often than not, I only hear a brief ticking sound, or a short rattle of a few notes delivered at breakneck speed. It is a sound easy to overlook, like the bird itself, yet once you learn that it is produced by the wren, it provides another important clue to its presence.

In our gardens, too, the wren is far less obvious at this time of year. The BTO's Garden BirdWatch survey, in which thousands of citizen scientists monitor the rises and falls in the numbers of birds in their garden throughout the seasons, shows that September is the lowest month for wren records. Bear in mind that the people doing this survey tend to be at the more expert end of the birding spectrum, and we can conclude that if wrens were there, they would probably record them.

There are two possible explanations for the reduction in wren numbers in early autumn. One is obvious: wrens, like many other small birds, are far easier to see during the spring and early summer – when they are either singing or bringing back food for their young – and also in the depths of winter, when they need to forage more actively for food. The other, perhaps more likely, reason is that – again like many other small garden birds – they have temporarily left our gardens to seek food in the wider neighbourhood.

September usually sees the peak of food supplies in the wider countryside, when there are plenty of fruits, nuts, berries – and for the wren, small insects. So, as I cycle around the lanes behind my home, I hear the tell-tale rattle of wrens from time to time, and often wonder if these are the birds that hatched out in my own garden just a few months earlier. And it also brings home to me the irony that our commonest bird has become so embedded in our literature and popular culture – when it is indeed so easy to overlook.

In Geoffrey Chaucer's early poem 'Court of Love' (almost certainly written when he was a young student at Cambridge), he makes a passing mention of the wren, which he says 'gan scippen and to daunce' (began to skip and dance).

Yet the first poetic reference to the wren in the English language may date from more than a century earlier. 'The Owl and the Nightingale', a long poem known only from two manuscripts (one at Jesus College, Oxford, the other in the British Library) was probably composed around 1250. It takes the form of a debate between the two titular birds, concerning which of them is most useful to mankind.

The wren makes an appearance towards the end of this epic 1,800-line poem, taking the side of the nightingale. The anonymous author credits the wren not only with a 'good, clear song' but also with wisdom, and a greater understanding of the human way of thinking than the other birds.

More than three centuries later, the wren is one of more than fifty different species of native and exotic bird mentioned in Shakespeare's plays, where it appears several times, in very different contexts. At the beginning of the closing act of *The Merchant of Venice*, the play's heroine Portia proclaims:

> The crow doth sing as sweetly as the lark
> When neither is attended, and I think
> The nightingale, if she should sing by day
> When every goose is cackling, would be thought
> No better a musician than the wren.

Elsewhere, Shakespeare appears to have taken a similarly negative view of the wren. Near the start of *Richard III*, the eponymous king laments that 'The world is grown so bad, that wrens make prey where eagles dare not perch.' And in *King Lear* there is a passing reference to the wren's reputation for promiscuity:

> . . .Die for adultery? No.
> The wren goes to 't, and the small gilded fly
> Does lecher in my sight. Let copulation thrive…

A more wholesome image can be found in *Twelfth Night*, where Sir Toby Belch refers to his lover and future wife Maria as 'the youngest Wren of nine', and also, as already mentioned, in *Macbeth*, when Lady Macduff unfavourably compares her absent husband to a male wren that defends its youngsters against the predatory owl.

After this, however, literary references to the wren are few and far between. In John Dryden's 1677 play *All for Love*, a retelling of Shakespeare's *Antony and Cleopatra*, Antony refers to the myth of the King of Birds:

> Fool that I was, upon my eagle's wings I bore this wren, till I was tired with soaring, and now he mounts above me.

The Romantic poets often wrote about birds, as we've already seen with Wordsworth's delightful lines on the wren's nesting place:

> This moss-lined shed, green, soft, and dry,
> Harbours a self-contented Wren.

But until John Clare, no literary figure had ever devoted an entire poem to this species.

Typically, Clare begins his sonnet with a sideswipe against his peers, for their devotion to more obvious birds and their songs:

> Why is the cuckoo's melody preferred
> And nightingale's rich song so fondly praised
> In poet's rhymes? Is there no other bird
> Of nature's minstrelsy that oft hath raised
> One's heart to extacy and mirth as well?

He then shifts gear to reflect on his own preferences for less celebrated species:

> I judge not how another's taste is caught:
> With mine, there's other birds that bear the bell
> Whose song hath crowds of happy memories brought.
> Such the wood-robin singing in the dell
> And little wren that many a time hath sought
> Shelter from showers in huts where I did dwell
> In early spring the tennant of the plain
> Tenting my sheep and still they come to tell
> The happy stories of the past again.

This is typical of Clare's championing of the common and familiar, against the more obvious poetic choices, notably the skylark and the nightingale.

Since John Clare was writing, around two centuries ago, few poets (apart from Ted Hughes, who wrote at least two wren poems) have placed the wren at the centre of their work. One notable exception was the Irish poet Michael Hartnett (also known as Mícheál Ó hairtnéide), who like Clare had his roots in the rural landscape – in his case Limerick.

His 1987 poem, 'A Necklace of Wrens', published in both Irish and English, has something of Clare's simplicity of language, and also reminds me of William Blake.

Another Irish poet, Michael Longley, also has a soft spot for wrens. In an interview in 2011 he referred to the power of the wren's 'monumental song . . . produced by a bird the size of a ping-pong ball'.

During the First World War, many serving soldiers found comfort in hearing the songs of familiar birds from home. The skylark and the nightingale tend to get the most mentions in this context, yet the wren was also occasionally reported.

In *Wings Over the Western Front*, the war diaries of Collingwood Ingram, the author makes several passing references to the autumn song of the wren, including this entry for 25 September 1918 near the village of

St-André: 'A wren was singing in a hedgerow very softly and its voice sounded very far away although the bird was actually not more than a few paces from me.'

Ingram was one of the lucky ones. Less than two months later, on 11 November, the Armistice was signed, and the 'war to end all wars' was finally over. Unharmed and alive – unlike many of his ornithological contemporaries – Ingram returned home to Kent, where he pursued a distinguished career as a horticulturalist and plant collector, becoming an expert on Japanese flowering cherries.

He also continued to make careful observations on, and drawings of, birds in Kent, finding the first pair of marsh warblers to nest in his home county. He was a member of the prestigious British Ornithologists' Union for eighty-one years – a record never beaten, before or since. Ingram died in May 1981, at the age of a hundred.

OCTOBER

Call for the robin-red-breast and the wren,

Since o'er shady groves they hover,

And with leaves and flowers do cover

The friendless bodies of unburied men.

John Webster, *The White Devil*,

Act V, Scene 4, 1612

On the south coast of England, as night begins to fall, a north-westerly wind is blowing. After rain earlier in the day, the sky has finally cleared, with the moon rising and the stars just beginning to appear. It's a perfect night for migration, and thousands – perhaps hundreds of thousands – of birds are on the move.

The shortest crossing from Britain to France is in south-east Kent. It runs from South Foreland, across the Straits of Dover, to the cliffs of Cap Gris Nez in France – a distance of some 33.3 km (almost 21 miles). This is the route favoured by Channel swimmers, and also by migrating birds.

Soon after dusk, they start to appear. Thrushes and blackbirds, robins and chats, warblers and flycatchers, all streaming steadily south, taking advantage of the light following winds. Some, like the willow warblers and whitethroats, will eventually fly all the way to sub-Saharan Africa; others, such as the chiffchaffs and blackcaps, don't go as far, spending the winter in Iberia or north-west Africa.

They travel under cover of darkness for two reasons. First, they are far less vulnerable to predators; and also, cooler temperatures enable them to fly faster, and for longer, than during the day. In twelve hours or so, when dawn breaks, they will land to feed and rest during daylight hours, before heading off again at dusk tomorrow night. By then, they will be far away from our shores – and they won't return for another six or seven months, when we welcome them back in the spring.

Not all of our birds join them; indeed, about two-thirds of Britain's breeding songbird species are sedentary, spending the whole year here. Some, like the house sparrow, rarely venture more than a mile or so from where they were born during the whole of their lifetime. Others, including the robin, are partial migrants, with some birds heading south in autumn while the majority stay put.

We usually think of the wren as entirely sedentary. This belief is re-inforced by the regular sight of wrens in our gardens during the autumn and winter months; and also, perhaps, because we cannot believe that they would be able to fly any real distance on those short, stubby wings.

Yet some British wrens do migrate – and travel a lot further than we might imagine. The BTO's *Winter Atlas*, based on fieldwork carried out in the early 1980s, confirmed that although most British wrens are indeed sedentary, or travel only short distances from their birthplace, a few more intrepid birds do cross the English Channel. Ringed birds have been re-trapped in France, Belgium and the Netherlands; but as so few ringed wrens are ever recovered – well under one per cent – the numbers crossing from Britain into continental Europe may be far higher than we think.

In the early 1970s, a study entitled 'Wren movements and survival', published in *British Birds*, analysed the distances travelled by the 378 wrens recovered from a grand total of just over 69,000 ringed in the UK.

The results confirmed that most wrens are not great travellers: 80 per cent were found less than five km from where they had been ringed, and a further 14 per cent had managed to travel between five

and 100 km. Only twenty-three birds – a mere six per cent – had travelled further than 100 km. And just seven had flown more than 250 km (about 160 miles) from their place of origin – three birds managing to reach the south of France, one as far as the Camargue. The main month of travel was October, though they can set off any time from August and September, coinciding with the peak of songbird migration.

But even quite sedentary wrens are more restless at this time of year, with a number of birds making more-or-less random movements, travelling less than 50 km from where they are born. Many of these were found roosting in reedbeds, and turned out to be mostly females. The authors of the paper, I. Hawthorn and C. J. Mead, concluded that these may have lost out to the more assertive and dominant males, at a time when they are beginning to establish their autumn and winter territories. Once the females had found a suitable reedbed, with enough food to sustain them through the cold weather, they often returned to the same site the following winter.

The authors speculated that this propensity of some wrens to disperse more or less randomly in autumn might have helped the species colonise Eurasia, as it would have allowed them to exploit suitable new regions more rapidly.

Some European wrens arrive in Britain at this time of year: a steady passage of continental birds has been observed along the east coast of England, often at lighthouses, which attract migrating birds confused by the powerful beam. These mainly come from Germany and Scandinavia: hardly unexpected, given that few small birds can survive the freezing winters in this part of Europe.

On Fair Isle, whose isolated geographical position acts as a magnet for migrating birds, there is a noticeable peak of wrens from mid-September to mid-October. These are not the local Fair Isle wren, whose population is both small and fairly constant, but come from the nominate race *troglodytes*, and have flown all the way across the North Sea from Norway.

Wrens that arrive during the autumn often do so at the same time as, or just ahead of, migrating woodcocks. For this reason, they (along with goldcrests) were once known in eastern England as the 'woodcock pilot'. It is often assumed that this was because they were supposed to ride on the backs of these secretive waders, steering them on their course across the sea. But as Alfred Newton explained in his 1893 *Dictionary of Birds*, the real reason is rather more prosaic:

The bird in autumn visits the east coast in enormous flocks. . . they are well known to the fishermen as 'Woodcock's Pilots', from their generally preceding by a few days the advent of those regular immigrants.

The ornithologist David Bannerman, whose magisterial twelve-volume work *The Birds of the British Isles* was published from 1953 to 1963, noted that there is a regular passage of wrens down both the western and eastern coasts of Scotland and England, including the Isle of May in the outer reaches of the Firth of Forth, east of Fife.

They were observed there by the redoubtable Misses Rintoul and Baxter. Always referred to as 'the good ladies', Leonora Rintoul and Evelyn Baxter were pioneers in the study of bird migration during the years either side of the Second World War, at a time when ornithology was very much a male-dominated calling. These two women were well able to hold their own, though, and were certainly not averse to shooting any rare bird they came across in order to identify it.

During the many years they studied birds on the Isle of May, they frequently came across migrant wrens, in both spring and autumn. But fortunately, when it came to the wren they knew what they were looking at, and so refrained from blasting these little birds to kingdom come.

Far to the south and west, in Ireland, the night of 16 October 1901 saw the greatest influx of wrens ever recorded. They appeared in large numbers, especially at lighthouses, all the way from the Fastnet Rock in the west to Rockabill, near Dublin, in the east – a stretch of coast roughly 430 km (270 miles) long. Another early student of bird migration, William Eagle Clarke, saw several at Eddystone Lighthouse, off the coast of south-east Cornwall, on the very same night.

The next morning, the corpses of no fewer than ten unfortunate wrens were found beneath the lighthouse at Tuskar Rock, off the coast of Wexford. As Bannerman observed, the migration of wrens was then, as now, far from common knowledge: 'That the tiny wren can make such journeys across the sea as a regular occurrence is not generally known, most people believing it incapable of sustained flight, but such is undoubtedly the case.'

Whether the birds seen in such high numbers in Ireland had flown across the Irish Sea in Britain, or had travelled there from much farther afield – perhaps northern Europe – we do not know, as this was before the days when birds were ringed.

The further north and east we go in Europe, the more likely it is that wrens will be entirely migratory. Indeed, once we reach the minus-seven-degree January isotherm, in the heart of Siberia, they are unable to survive the winter, and have no choice but to head south and west to take advantage of the milder, more maritime climate in western Europe. And in doing so, they may travel considerable distances.

The most incredible journey of all was that of a wren ringed at Rybachy, on the Baltic Sea close to Russia's border with Lithuania, on 3 September 1996. The following March it was found, long dead, in West Sussex – no less than 1,524 km (more than 950 miles) from where it had been ringed. And don't forget, it may well have travelled from much further east before it was trapped at the site where it was ringed.

Meanwhile, in woods and gardens throughout the British Isles, the vast majority of wrens are settling down to prepare for the winter to come.

Like robins, these resident birds hold autumn and winter territories, and sing to defend them – though to me the regular singing of wrens throughout the colder months of the year feels like a fairly recent phenomenon. I can still recall, some time early on in the millennium, returning late one evening to the BBC Natural History Unit's Bristol HQ, and being surprised to hear a wren singing, well past midnight, perhaps encouraged by the lights of the car park.

Yet autumnal singing must have been going on for far longer than I recall, because two centuries ago William Wordsworth observed that on breezy days in autumn,

> To the wind she [sic] sometimes gives
> A slender, unexpected strain.

But at this time of year, as the days get shorter, a wren may not be able to spare any time for the luxury of song, as it will be mainly preoccupied with finding food. The early twentieth-century ornithologist Edmund Selous (the man who, in the title of his 1901 book, coined the phrase *Bird Watching*) observed a wren feeding in a grove of 'Scotch firs' (presumably Scots pines) one October day: 'A wren flew to and commenced to ascend perpendicularly the trunk of a tree quite near me, flying thence to another which it also ascended, and so on from tree to tree.'

Selous also observed blue tits behaving in the same manner, and concluded: 'Both the blue-tit, therefore, and the wren have acquired the habit of creeping about the trunks of trees, in search, presumably, of insects or spiders, as do the tree-creepers, woodpeckers, and nut-hatch.'

On another occasion, in February, Selous again saw a wren behaving 'just like a professional tree-creeper'.

ÉIRE 40
51c

Troglodytes troglodytes

Wren   Dreoilín

It ascended the trunk of an alder, quickly and easily, and sometimes
to a considerable height – twenty or thirty feet perhaps – beginning
from the roots, and then flew down to the base or roots of the next
one, and so on along a whole line of them. Up the sloping roots,
or anywhere at all horizontal, it hopped along in the usual manner,
but, when the trunk became perpendicular, it crept or crawled, just
like a true tree-creeper.

With the breeding season now some distance behind and ahead of us,
October is also the time when conservationists and bird ringers put out
nest boxes, including those for wrens. The naturalist, author and wildlife
filmmaker Ben Macdonald points out that because wrens are capable of
nesting almost anywhere, and are so adaptable when it comes to choos-

ing a site, putting up boxes to try to attract them can be very hit-and-miss – in some years, hardly any of them are occupied the following spring.

But when he and some colleagues were putting up nest boxes in the Malvern Hills, on the Worcestershire-Herefordshire border, they discovered the solution to their problem: entirely by accident, as he explains.

We had often found wrens breeding in old swallow nests. Wrens and swallows have been neighbours for hundreds of thousands, perhaps millions of years, so that wasn't enormously surprising. Being able to steal your neighbour's nest, while they're away in Africa for the winter, is the kind of genius that has made wrens so successful.

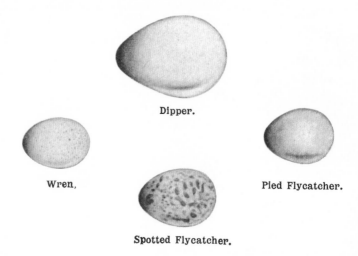

Dipper.

Wren.

Pied Flycatcher.

Spotted Flycatcher.

But Ben wasn't prepared for what happened when the owner of the orchard where they were studying the wrens decided to put up some concrete, bowl-shaped nest boxes, specifically designed to attract swallows when they returned from Africa the following spring. Instead, wrens moved straight in, having found a way to squeeze their domed nests into the swallow boxes, giving the ringers a really easy way to monitor them the following breeding season.

Swallows weren't the only wild creatures ejected by these tiny squatters, as Ben recalls.

In nearby woods, we also learned that whilst wrens almost never used a conventional nest box with a hole, they often used dormice boxes. They would enter around the back, between the trunk and the little mouse hole in the back of the box. Clearly this gave them more protection, as they could squeeze through a smaller gap than most curious blue tits.

Of course, we've found dozens of wren nests in natural situations, from missing bricks to wood piles, and they seem particularly fond of nesting low in bramble and gorse. But to get a wren to nest to order, a fake swallow nest, or a dormouse box, is a pretty good place to start.

NOVEMBER

You cannot fly like an eagle with the wings of a wren.

W. H. Hudson

Thomas Hood, the nineteenth-century poet and humourist, got it pretty well right when he wrote this short, sharp verse about the year's penultimate month:

> No sun – no moon!
> No morn – no noon –
> No dawn – no dusk – no proper time of day.
> No warmth, no cheerfulness, no healthful ease,
> No comfortable feel in any member –
> No shade, no shine, no butterflies, no bees,
> No fruits, no flowers, no leaves, no birds! –
> November!

To most naturalists, November is the low point of the year. Summer is so far behind us as to be merely a distant memory; but spring is still several months ahead. And before then, we must suffer the slow, steady decline of daylight leading up to the winter solstice towards the dying days of the year.

For small birds such as the wren, November can be a tricky month, too. By now, any birds that were going to move a few miles down the road – or perhaps further – have already done so, and virtually all wrens are now living in the place where they will spend the whole of the winter.

At this time of year, only the robin sings regularly, though wrens do occasionally burst into song, as if rehearsing for the breeding season to come. But they will only get that far if they are able to find enough food to survive the winter; and with both food resources, and the time available to feed, now limited, that can be very tricky.

Like many small birds, wrens change their behaviour considerably as winter begins to bite. They rarely join forces with other species, in the manner of tits, goldcrests and treecreepers, which form loose feeding flocks in which every bird helps the others by calling continuously as they travel through the forest canopy. Unlike these species, which are just as fiercely territorial during the breeding season, wrens do not really do 'sociability'.

Yet as Dominic Couzens points out in *The Secret Lives of Garden Birds*:

> Even highly-strung wrens gather in small spaces to sleep alongside their congeners. . . It is not their normal practice; they much prefer to roost alone. But in fear of their lives wrens huddle together, sometimes in several layers in a confined space, with each bird facing inward.

It must take a lot for such a solitary, independent bird as a wren to roost communally like this. But desperate times call for desperate measures. Yet as soon as they finish roosting together they pursue their individual lives once again, vigorously defending their territory during daylight hours, before coming together with their rivals each evening.

For such a common bird, the roosting habits of the wren have rarely

been studied; even Edward Armstrong struggled to find a roost where he was able to observe the birds. He did discover that, as is frequent amongst songbirds, female wrens tend to retire to the roost earlier in the evening, and leave later in the morning, than the males. He also noted that wrens have a remarkable memory for their roosting sites, being able to recall the exact location several months after their previous visit.

During one particularly cold spell, he noticed that his local wrens would do a tour of the area, as if searching out both a place to spend the night and 'potential bedfellows' to join forces with. He even suggested that wrens will take part in a kind of 'follow-my-leader', in which one bird – presumably a mature individual with experience of previous cold snaps – guides the others to the best roosting site, calling frequently to attract their attention. That has been confirmed by modern observers, who have also watched males flying in and out of the roosting place to attract the others' attention.

But having arrived at their home for the night, the wren's confrontational nature sometimes leads to fights between two or more individuals. And as the first signs of spring appear, resident males will sometimes try to stop their rivals from entering the roost site, but still allow females – as potential mates – to come in.

Armstrong recounted the story of one particular roosting wren, which was observed by Mrs Winifred Moreau, the wife and colleague of ornithologist Reg Moreau, and the inspiration behind another of my books (*Mrs Moreau's Warbler: How Birds Got Their Names*). During the bitter winter of 1946/47, having returned from Africa, where they had lived for many years, the Moreaus were temporarily living in the village of Madingley, just outside Cambridge.

One evening, a wren appeared outside the room where Winnie Moreau was sitting, and tapped on the window-pane. Then it flew around the house to the other side and did exactly the same thing on the window opposite. It later transpired that, according to the house's previous owner, wrens from his garden would regularly enter the house to roost, taking advantage of the warmth and safety it provided. The polar explorer Antony Jinman has also observed similar behaviour at his home in South Devon, where wrens occasionally enter the house at night and roost on the wooden rafters in his sitting-room.

Wrens also frequently sleep in old nests – either their own, or those belonging to other species of bird – and have even been observed joining treecreepers, which often roost by clinging to the inside of a hollow in a

Wellingtonia tree (the huge conifer from North America also known as the giant redwood).

And just as wrens often nest in odd places, they sleep there too. They have been recorded roosting in reedbeds, haystacks, tree hollows, in an old coconut shell and even perched on a nail inside an outbuilding. In summer they continue to roost at night but, as Armstrong put it, they 'do not require such cosy roosting-places . . . [and] are much less inclined to return night after night to the same recess'.

The pugnacious nature of wrens is illustrated from this eyewitness account of a wren roost made by my former colleague, wildlife cameraman Mark Payne-Gill. During the past three decades, Mark has travelled all over the world, and filmed some of the most incredible wildlife spectacles on the planet, including a humpback whale feeding frenzy for *Blue Planet 2*, and leaping baby geese for David Attenborough's series *Life*. Yet he still recalls a memorable incident from very early in his career, when he was filming a wren roost for the RSPB's Film Unit.

On a freezing midwinter's afternoon in 1990, Mark was sent down to Colchester in Essex, to check out reports of wrens roosting in a disused swallow's nest, situated on the corner of a garage built onto a suburban bungalow.

I arrived well before sunset, and the first thing I noticed was that wrens were already beginning to appear. At first, they skulked around the nest area, but then they flew up to the fence and began singing quite boldly. Soon afterwards, they went quiet, and one by one they sneaked into the nest, until after a few minutes they were all safely tucked up inside.

Mark had filmed the brief period of action, so was about to pack up his camera kit, when he heard noises from inside the nest. These got louder and louder, and more and more tetchy in tone, until suddenly one of the wrens flew out, swiftly followed by the others.

What I found really intriguing was that even though the temperature was well below zero, these birds had not only emerged from their warm roosting place, but had then started singing again. By then it was almost dark, yet they were puffing their chests out, spreading their wings and throwing their heads back to sing as loudly as they could.

After another five or ten minutes, all went quiet again, and the wrens began to go back into the nest.

It was as if they were getting so cold they had finally realised that they needed to rely on each other – so stopped arguing! But then, to my astonishment, they started squabbling again; then they all piled out for a second time, like something out of a kids' cartoon. They then had another 'sing-off' on the fence; and all piled back. This happened several times, until after about an hour, when it was dark, they finally went back into the nest for the last time and went to sleep. The whole incident seemed to me to sum up the wren's amazingly pugnacious personality!

Like all small birds, wrens are constantly on the look-out for danger. In some ways they are better off than many other species, which tend to stay in one spot to feed. When blackbirds and thrushes feed on windfall apples, or tits and finches gather on hanging feeders, they make themselves a sitting target for cats and sparrowhawks; whereas the wren, which seemingly never stops, is harder to target.

One study of the victims of sparrowhawks, conducted by the Nobel Prize-winning ethologist Niko Tinbergen, found just two wrens amongst a total of well over a thousand prey items. During Armstrong's own study, he never found a single wren carcass at a sparrowhawk's nest during the three years when this predator was present. And despite the reference to wrens defending their young against owls in Shakespeare's *Macbeth*, there are few records of owls taking either young or adult wrens.

As the *British Birds* paper on 'Wren movements and survival' revealed, predators are nevertheless a significant factor in the mortality of wrens. Starting with 378 ringed birds, when we discount those re-trapped alive by other bird ringers (just twenty-eight), and those reported simply as 'found dead', with no cause of death known (well over half the records), we are left with 142 birds.

Of these, almost two-thirds were killed by predators, with the rest being the victims of traffic – an occupational hazard for such a low-flying bird. Of the ninety-two birds taken by a predator, just four were killed by native species – a kestrel, a jay, an owl (the species not known) and a weasel. All the rest were caught and killed by our most lethal non-native predator, the domestic cat. In another study, published in the BTO's *Migration Atlas* in 2002, roughly half of all known deaths were attributable to cats, while a further third were caused by other human factors, such as collisions with windows.

These figures should perhaps be regarded with caution: after all, many cats bring their victims indoors to present to their owners, so such deaths are more likely to be reported. Yet it is still clear that, as with the robin and many other treasured garden birds, cats are a significant factor in their mortality. This is not least because in our gardens they occur at far higher densities than any natural predator.

If a cat does catch a wren – and the victims are usually the less experienced youngsters – it will often eat it, whereas cats rarely eat robins. It has been suggested that birds with a more cryptic plumage, like the wren, are more palatable than colourful ones. So the advantage of being better camouflaged may be outweighed by being tastier.

The weather – and its effects on the availability of food – is also clearly a major influence on the life expectancy of wrens, and probably accounts for the majority of those ringing recoveries where the cause of death is unknown.

At the first sign of a cold spell, wrens in and around gardens often become easier to see, because they take advantage of our homes and outbuildings, as this observation from Thomas Bewick, writing at the very end of the eighteenth century, shows:

> This active little bird . . . braves our severest winters. . . During that
> season it approaches near the dwellings of man, and takes shelter
> in the roofs of houses, barns and in hay-stacks; it sings till late in
> the evening, and not unfrequently during a fall of snow.

But what of wrens living and breeding elsewhere, in the wider countryside? A 1995 study of wrens living in one Nottinghamshire wood, carried out over two decades, revealed that following the two harsh winters of 1978/79 and 1985/86, 'all or almost all birds which had previously bred

in the wood probably died.' It seemed that snowy winters are worse for wrens than other, very cold ones, with little or no snow: which makes sense, given that wrens usually feed on or near the ground, so if snow covers up their food they are more likely to starve.

I do wonder why – since cold, snowy weather so reduces their chances of survival – wrens don't just follow the example of species such as the lapwing, fieldfare and redwing. All of these birds regularly flee ahead of the arrival of cold weather, often heading south and west, or even crossing over to France, to avoid it.

Yet it appears that, even in very bad winters, most wrens prefer to take their chances on their own, familiar territory, where they know how to find food, rather than heading off into the unknown. Put simply, it pays to stay put rather than flee.

However, wrens that breed at any kind of altitude almost always travel a short distance down to more productive lowland areas in autumn. At one site in lowland Kent, just 60 metres (roughly 200 feet) above sea level, the ornithologist Jim Flegg reported that most wrens were resident throughout the year; whereas at his colleague Chris Mead's ringing site on the Chilterns, wrens breeding 200 metres (650 feet) above sea level mostly left for lower altitudes, where food was presumably more plentiful and easier to find, and snow less likely to settle.

In *Somerset Birds*, published in 1943, E. W. Hendy included his observations of the few songbird species that remained on Exmoor during the winter months. Surprisingly, perhaps, these included the wren:

> Even in the severest weather the indomitable wren clings to the bleak moors. The hardihood of these diminutive birds, which are among the smallest we possess in England, is astonishing. When everything is covered with snow, one never fails to find them among the heather and gorse so high as 1000, and up to 1300 and 1400 feet [400 to 430 metres].

Hendy goes on to explain how the wren takes advantage of its small size to survive in this desolate, windswept and unproductive habitat:

> Snow rarely presses deep heather quite flat; there are always some interstices, and this is, of course, true to an even greater extent of gorse. Creeping among the undergrowth, this mouse-like little creature contrives to find something to eat when larger birds, like the more delicate redwing, are found frozen to death under the clump of ling which has proved to be their last refuge.

He also closely observed the wren's feeding strategy in cold weather:

I have often watched him scuttering and fluttering along the crumbled banks of a partly frozen water-course, peering into every cranny, and seeking out the trifles which serve to sustain vitality in his small but sturdy body. . . 'Never say die' might be his motto, and that indeed is the motif of his cheery song – so large in volume for so small a bird – which bursts out irrepressibly on the smallest provocation in the dullest and most depressing of winter days.

Now that we rarely experience the kind of long, cold winters that were regular during the middle decades of the twentieth century, it is hard for us to imagine the effects of these prolonged spells of freezing weather on birds like the wren. But during Edward Armstrong's lifetime, such harsh winters occurred roughly every decade or so. He reported many instances of wrens dying in cold weather, including several found dead under the old nests in which they were roosting, the morning after a very cold night.

The winters of 1916/17, 1928/29, 1939/40, 1946/47 and especially the 'Big Freeze' of 1962/63, had a devastating short-term effect on many songbirds. Being so small and light, so sedentary in nature, and so reliant on a ready supply of small insects, the wren suffered more than most.

Following two successive colder-than-average winters in the early 1960s, 1961/62 and 1962/63, between seventy-eight per cent and ninety per cent of Britain's wrens failed to survive. This placed the wren fifth in the list of the hardest-hit species (the kingfisher and grey wagtail, both of which rely on unfrozen watercourses, were hit the hardest). Yet in less than a decade, wren numbers were back to their pre-crisis level.

The same appears to be true of later cold winters, notably 1978/79, 1984/85 and 1985/86, and most recently 2009/10 and 2010/11. None of these have led to a long-term reduction in wren numbers, or threatened its apparently unassailable position as Britain's commonest bird.

In 2016, new research by BTO scientists revealed that some populations of wrens have a built-in defence mechanism against cold weather: their slightly larger size. It's not just the island races of the wren that are bigger and bulkier than their mainland cousins: there is also a smaller – but still significant – difference in their size from north to south.

The *Guardian*'s headline, 'Why bigger is better, for a Scottish wren', pretty much summed up the study's findings. Long-term data collected by volunteers showed that wrens in south-west Britain have a body mass on average roughly five per cent lower than those in north-east Scotland.

For some birds, this extra weight proved to be the difference between life and death. Even though wrens in Scotland experienced up to seventy per cent more days of ground frost (a clear indicator of severe weather), they were still marginally more likely to survive through the winter than their southern relatives.

If that is the case, then why don't those soft southern wrens put on a few grams, to increase their chances of surviving? Partly because they don't have to, as winters there are usually mild. But another reason is because extra body mass can come with drawbacks. Being larger may help you get through a cold snap, but it also makes you less agile, and so potentially less able to escape from a predator.

This brings us to one of the most important factors facing all wildlife, anywhere in the world: global climate change. While it is very difficult to speculate on what effects this will have on our birds, in general it is likely that common, widespread and highly adaptable species such as the wren will continue to do well, while rare, restricted and highly specialised species will not.

Currently the wren breeds across a very wide range of geographical and climatic zones. In Europe alone, it can be found from the southern tip of Spain, at roughly thirty-six degrees north of the Equator, all the way up to the Varanger Peninsula in Norway, which lies some way beyond the Arctic Circle, at over seventy degrees North.

In 2007, the authors of *A Climatic Atlas of European Breeding Birds* attempted a bold experiment. They fed data on bird distribution and numbers into a computer, and used it to produce maps of the current range of each species. They then added data showing predicted rises in temperature, and produced a new map showing what they called the 'simulated potential late twenty-first-century distribution' of each species. This was based on informed speculation on where a species might live in a world altered by climate change.

For many birds, including the wren, the results predicted a reduction of range in the southern parts of Europe which, if forecasts of long-term temperature rises prove correct, will be turned into large swathes of desert or semi-desert. These losses in the south were at least partly balanced by range extensions in the north of Europe. Astonishingly, it was even suggested that, by the year 2100, wrens will be breeding on the archipelago of Svalbard (often known as Spitsbergen).

Lying between seventy-four and eighty-one degrees North – just over 1,000 kilometres (625 miles) from the North Pole – Svalbard currently boasts just one regular breeding species of songbird: the snow bunting. That the wren might join it there, within less than a century, is both a tribute to the adaptability of this little bird, and a dire warning against impending environmental catastrophe.

CARL DO...

DECEMBER

'O where are you going?' said Milder to Maulder.

'O we may not tell you,' said Festle to Foes.

'We're off to the woods,' said John the Red Nose.

'What will you do there?' said Milder to Maulder.

'O we may not tell you,' said Festle to Foes.

'We'll hunt the Cutty Wren,' said John the Red Nose.

Traditional Folk Song

They gathered at daybreak, on St Stephen's Day, 26 December. Dressed in a curious array of clothing – including women's dresses and makeshift helmets – and carrying a variety of homemade musical instruments and sticks, they were quiet at first. Still rubbing sleep from their eyes, and nursing a Christmas hangover from the excesses of the night before, many groused and grumbled at the early start.

But as the milky winter sunshine began to seep through the mist across the fields around the village, they began to brighten up, and the moans and groans turned to excited anticipation of what lay ahead.

This motley bunch were known as the Wren Boys, after the tiny target they had gathered to find. For this was the Wren Hunt, an ancient tradition in theirs and countless other villages across Ireland.

In a cross between a treasure hunt and the American custom of 'trick-or-treat', these young men and boys headed off in pursuit of the unfortunate wren, working their way along the field boundaries around the outskirts of their village, and banging the hedgerows with sticks.

Finally, they caught the poor bird, which was then tied to the end of a pole, and later placed in a cage adorned with evergreen leaves such as holly and ivy, along with decorative ribbons. But catching the wren was just the start: once they had done so, they paraded the incarcerated bird through the village streets, singing traditional songs. The actual lyrics of these, if not the sentiments, varied from place to place, but one version went like this:

> The wren, the wren, the king of all birds,
> St Stephen's Day was caught in the furze,
> Although he was little his honour was great,
> Jump up me lads and give him a treat.

As the Wren Boys sang, they knocked on doors and demanded food and drink, sometimes in exchange for the bird's tiny feathers, which were supposed to be a lucky charm (though not, perhaps, for the unfortunate wren, which towards the end of the day might be almost bald). An alternative final couplet to the verse makes these requests more explicit:

> Come, give us a bumper [a cup of wine], or give us a cake,
> Or give us a copper, for charity's sake.

At last, having exhausted the patience and hospitality of their neighbours, the Wren Boys carried the caged bird to the churchyard, where it was either stoned to death – to commemorate the fate of St Stephen, the earliest Christian martyr (who met his death by stoning the year after Jesus's crucifixion) – or simply killed and then buried, with great ceremony, in the ground.

The Victorian ornithologist William Yarrell wrote a vivid account of the proceedings:

On Christmas-day boys and men, each using two sticks, one to beat the bushes, the other to fling at the bird, went out in a body to hunt and kill the wren, which from its habit of making short flights was no doubt soon done to death. On the following day, the feast of St Stephen, the dead bird, hung by the leg between two hoops, crossed at right angles and decked with ribbons, was carried about by the 'wren-boys', who sang a song . . . and begged money to bury the wren.

Edward Armstrong had also observed the Wren Hunt at first hand, and was clearly not a great enthusiast for the event:

The Wren Hunt is among the most elaborate bird rituals surviving in Europe and is best preserved in the British Isles, though the casual observer of some of the present-day jollifications might not be greatly impressed. In an Irish village on St Stephen's Day (26 December) he might see a tumultuous party of lads dressed in ludicrous garments, such as pyjama jackets and women's blouses, some with faces blackened, going from house to house, stopping here and there to sing a few doggerel lines and to collect a coin from the householders.

There are many theories behind the origins of this bizarre tradition. Some say that in the distant past, when the Irish were at war with their enemies from across the water, a wren betrayed them by tapping on a drum as it sang, thus revealing their whereabouts.

The enemies in this tale vary from place to place: some versions suggest that they were Vikings, which would date the story's origins to well before the Norman Conquest; others claim they were the forces of Oliver Cromwell, who invaded and subjugated Ireland in the early 1650s; or the army of the Protestant King William of Orange, who went to war with the Catholic supporters of King James II of England (James VII of Scotland) from 1688 to 1691.

In other versions, the origin of the custom goes back even further. The wren is said to have betrayed St Stephen when, just before his execution, he attempted to escape: the bird is meant to have flown into the face of one of his sleeping jailers and woken him up. It has also been suggested that the wren was hunted down because it was in fact a beautiful fairy disguised as a bird and, if it were allowed to sing, it would lure its unwitting victims to a watery grave.

Although usually associated with rural Ireland, the Wren Hunt is also known from south-west Scotland, Wales, the Isle of Man, and parts of southern England: indeed, Armstrong suggests that it may have its origins on this side of the Irish Sea. The tradition was even found as far south as the ancient fortified town of Carcassonne in south-west France. Here, the hunt took place from the first to the last Sunday in December, in what was known as the *Fête du Roitelet* ('the little king's fair'). In a grisly twist to the tradition, the wren would be impaled on the end of a pole before being paraded around the town.

As with many traditional customs, its adherents have claimed that the Wren Hunt has its origins in pre-Christian, pagan folklore, going back several millennia. In his 1958 book *The Folklore of Birds*, Edward Armstrong suggested that the various beliefs surrounding the wren – which he lumped under the umbrella term 'the Wren Cult' – reached these islands during the Bronze Age (roughly 2500 to 800 BC).

For him, the wren represented 'new year ceremonial having as its

A jolly
Christmas
to you.

I wish you a Ricky Christmas
Pot luck no doubt you'll say,
But birdies think it the best of luck
They have no rent to pay.

purpose the defeat of the dark-earth powers and identification with the hoped-for triumph of light and life'. However, a trawl through parish records in Britain and Ireland has failed to find any evidence that it actually occurred before the late seventeenth century.

Whatever its origins, during the nineteenth and twentieth centuries, as we became more sensitive to the welfare of birds and other wild creatures, and as old customs began to decline, the hunt either died out or was changed into a ritual ceremony.

This appears to have happened first in France, where it was frowned on by the revolutionaries, revived when the monarchy was restored in 1814 (following the defeat of Napoleon), and then banned again in the

1830s. As the nineteenth century went on, and the notion that we should not be cruel to animals grew more popular, the Wren Hunt also fell out of favour in many parts of Britain. One early advocate of animal rights, William H. Drummond, roundly condemned the ritual: 'What shall we think of the "most diminutive of birds"; being hunted and stoned, for a supposed political offence of one or two of its progenitors above seven-score years before it was born?'

However, despite his protestations, the Wren Hunt continued to take place in some parts of Britain and Ireland well into the twentieth century. One elderly resident of the Isle of Man, interviewed by Elizabeth Atwood Lawrence in *Hunting the Wren*, recalled the events of his childhood – some time around the First World War – with great nostalgia:

By the time we were twelve or thirteen, we thought we were too grown up to do it. But when we were little, all the children looked forward to it. We made two wooden hoops, like a cross, decorated with streamers and with artificial flowers at the top. I went from house to house and usually got a penny. We sang and recited the words to the wren song when we knocked on the door, and sometimes collected a shilling or two.

But by then, the ceremony had mostly become a purely ritual one, with the wren's life spared:

We didn't kill a wren, though. My father . . . often went hunting, and killed hares, partridges and grouse, but he wouldn't shoot that little bird, he wouldn't kill a wren.

Today, a version of the Wren Hunt still persists in the Isle of Man, and also in Ireland, in the counties of Kerry, Cork and Limerick. But nowadays, thanks to bird protection laws and a more enlightened attitude, the ceremony does not end with the wren being captured or killed: instead, the cage or box is empty, or contains a fake bird.

According to Mark Cocker's encyclopaedic collection of avian folklore *Birds Britannica*, participants in these events (at least until the early part of the millennium, when his book was published) would often wear masks of Margaret Thatcher, 'a measure of [her] enduring status as a hate figure in Irish society'.

So, what should we make of this collection of stories and superstitions that together make up the Wren Hunt? Ultimately, it combines a powerful blend of ancient superstition, pagan symbolism, Christian beliefs, animal sacrifice, our propensity to ascribe special powers to birds and, last but not least, a widespread desire amongst rural people to join together and have a jolly good time. Indeed, I am inclined to side with Mark Cocker, when he concludes: '[The Wren Hunt] is – and perhaps always was – a vehicle for seasonal fun and games, rather than the continuation of a lost pagan rite.'

With so many (often contradictory) explanations of its origins and meaning, it is impossible to draw any overarching conclusions. Perhaps the last word should go to Elizabeth Atwood Lawrence, from the concluding paragraph of her thoughtful and forensically detailed book:

Today's citizens of the urbanised world typically have little or no direct interaction with wild nature. In contrast, pre-industrial people acquired intimate knowledge about the animals in their

Wren Boys' procession, Athea, Limerick, 1946

vicinity from daily experience. The original wren hunters knew a great deal about the habits of the mysterious bird they pursued and about its relatedness to the environment in which it lived.

Back in my Somerset garden, the year is drawing to a close. A chill wind has arrived from the north, bringing one or two brief flurries of snow, which are threatening to settle.

Just as dusk begins to fall, though, I hear a familiar sound: a wren's 'dance of rainbows', announcing to any listeners that this is indeed – in the words of Robert Wilson Lynd – 'the best of all possible worlds'.

It may still be a long time until spring comes to my corner of the West Country. But with its gung-ho attitude, so perfectly expressed in that brief but unmistakable cacophony of sound, this particular wren seems to be saying: 'Bring it on!'

EPILOGUE

From time to time, our deeply held connections with the wren re-surface, often at the most unexpected moments. In a *Sunday Times* feature published in January 2018, the palliative care doctor Rachel Clarke wrote movingly about the death from cancer of her father, Dr Mark Rendall, the previous Boxing Day:

> The morning after it happens, it is hard to believe the sun still shines. I am standing in the kitchen, staring out across fields of frost, when a wren darts and whirrs through the hedge in front of me. Dad, in a flash, is there too. 'Look, Rachel! A wren!' His heart, like mine, never failed to lift at this smallest and most jaunty of birds. But, the night before, cancer finally claimed my dad. The wrens will keep whirring, but he has gone.

At times of great emotional trauma and stress, we continue to find solace in the smallest of things. And few things are as small – and yet as powerful – as the sight of a wren, as it passes momentarily through our space, its life intersecting briefly with ours before it vanishes once again back into its own secret world.

May this little bird continue to comfort us, intrigue us, and above all delight us, for the rest of our lives.

ACKNOWLEDGEMENTS

Once again, I'd like to thank the team at Square Peg (an imprint of Penguin Random House): Rowan Yapp, who commissioned the book and ably steered it through the whole process of publication; Harriet Dobson, Madeleine Hartley and Nick Skidmore in Editorial; Helen Flood in Publicity; and the designers and production team, including picture researcher Lily Richards, led by Design Director Suzanne Dean, who always make my books look so good. The stunning cover image is by the doyen of bird illustrators, Robert Gillmor.

My friends Kevin and Donna Cox once again kindly allowed me to use their home as a writing retreat. Graham Coster edited the book with his usual blend of finesse, skill and perception, while my agent Broo Doherty was a great support, as ever.

My colleague at Bath Spa University, Gail Simmons, read the text and made several helpful suggestions, while my old friend Donald S. Murray and another Bath Spa colleague, Siân Melangell Dafydd, contributed stories from Scottish and Welsh folklore. Polly Pullar, Antony Jinman, Ben Macdonald and Mark Payne-Gill also shared stories of their own encounters with these little birds. And Dr Rachel Clarke kindly allowed me to quote from her piece about her father, Dr Mark Rendall, and his love of wrens.

A big thanks to my former student on Bath Spa University's MA in Travel and Nature Writing, Steven Lovatt, who gave me permission to reprint his wonderfully inventive poem, which captures the wren's spirit so well, as the book's epigraph. Thanks too to Katie Marland who provided the illustration for the poem.

Finally, I'd like to pay tribute to the man who knew and understood the wren better than anyone: the late Revd Edward A. Armstrong. His Collins New Naturalist monograph on the species is an extraordinary achievement by an essentially amateur naturalist, inspiring me as I was writing this book.

BIBLIOGRAPHY

Armstrong, Edward A., *The Wren*, London: Collins New Naturalist monograph, 1955

Armstrong, Edward A., *The Folklore of Birds*, London: Collins New Naturalist, 1958

Armstrong, Patrick, *The English Parson-Naturalist*, Leominster: Gracewing, 2000

Brewer, David, *Wrens, Dippers and Thrashers*, London: Christopher Helm, 2001

del Hoyo, J., Elliott, A. & Christie, D.A., eds. *Handbook of the Birds of the World: Vol. 10, Cuckoo-shrikes to Thrushes*, Barcelona: Lynx Edicions, 2005

Lawrence, Elizabeth Atwood, *Hunting the Wren: Transformation of Bird to Symbol*, Knoxville: University of Tennessee Press, 1997

Mac Coitir, Niall, *Ireland's Birds: Myths, Legends and Folklore*, Wilton, Cork: The Collins Press, 2015

LIST OF ILLUSTRATIONS

LIST OF ILLUSTRATIONS

p.48 *Passeriformes, couple of Winter Wren (Troglodytes troglodytes), courtship, male presenting nest to female* / Private Collection / De Agostini Picture Library / Bridgeman Images

p.50 Wren nesting in coat pocket from *The Wren* by Edward A. Armstrong (London: Collins, 1955)

p.52 Egg sketch from *British Birds' Eggs and Nests, Popularly Described* by Rev. J. C. Atkinson (London: Routledge, 1862).

p.60 *The Wren* (chromolitho), Lydon, Alexander Francis (1836-1917) / Private Collection / © Look and Learn / Bridgeman Images

p.65 1945 farthing featuring the wren

p.68 *Wren*, English School, (20th century) / Private Collection / © Look and Learn / Bridgeman Images

p.75 Wren feeding its young from *Birds and Their Young* by T.A. Coward (London: Gay & Hancock Ltd, 1923)

p.77 *Wren*. Wills's cigarette card, early 20th century. (English School, (20th century) / Private Collection / © Look and Learn / Bridgeman Images)

p.78 Wren with its nest and egg from The Pocket Guide to *Nests and Eggs* by R.S.R. Fitter (London: Collins, 1904)

p.80 *Troglodytes Europaeus - Common Wren*, Gould, John (1804-81) / Brooklyn Museum of Art, New York, USA / Gift of the Estate of Emily Winthrop Miles / Bridgeman Images

p.86 *The Cuckoo* (engraving), English School, (19th century) / Private Collection / © Look and Learn / Bridgeman Images

p.89 Sketch of wrens building a nest from *British Birds With Their Nests and Eggs* by Arthur G. Butler (Bumby & Clarke, London, 1896)

p.91 Wren watercolour from *British Birds in Their Haunts* by Rev. C.A. Johns (London: Routledge, 1910)

p.92 Female wren lining her nest from *The Wren* by Edward A. Armstrong (London: Collins, 1955)

p.94 *The Marriage* (chromolitho), English School, (19th century) / Private Collection / © Look and Learn / Bridgeman Images

LIST OF ILLUSTRATIONS

FIGS.	73—75	COAL-TIT.	FIGS.	91	PIED WAGTAIL.	FIGS.	102	ROCK-PIPIT.
	76—77	MARSH-TIT.		92	WHITE WAGTAIL.		103	GOLDEN ORIOLE.
	78—81	BLUE TIT.		93	GREY WAGTAIL.		104—108	RED-BACKED SHRIKE.
	82	CRESTED TIT.		94	BLUE-HEADED WAGTAIL.		109	WOODCHAT SHRIKE.
	83—84	NUTHATCH.		95—96	YELLOW WAGTAIL.		110	PIED FLYCATCHER.
	85—87	WREN.		97—100	TREE-PIPIT.		111—113	SPOTTED FLYCATCHER.
	88—90	TREE CREEPER.		101	MEADOW-PIPIT.			